Editor
Rita Seho

Editorial Project Manager
Ina Massler Levin, M.A.

Editor-in-Chief
Sharon Coan, M.S. Ed.

Illustrator
Agi Palinay

Cover Artist
Judy Walker

Art Coordinator
Cheri Macoubrie Wilson

Associate Designer
Denise Bauer

Art Director
Elayne Roberts

Imaging
Ralph Olmedo, Jr.

Product Manager
Phil Garcia

Publishers
Rachelle Cracchiolo, M.S. Ed.
Mary Dupuy Smith, M.S. Ed.

NEWSPAPER
Scavenger Hunts

Author

Tom Burt

Teacher Created Materials, Inc.
6421 Industry Way
Westminster, CA 92683
www.teachercreated.com
©1999 Teacher Created Materials, Inc.
Reprinted, 2004
ISBN-1-57690-353-2
Made in U.S.A.

Table of Contents

Table of Contents *(cont.)*

Introduction

Newspaper Scavenger Hunts

Newspaper Scavenger Hunts are enjoyable activities that can be incorporated into your classroom curriculum or used as Friday afternoon lessons. Before you begin, have students bring in newspapers from home. If students are unable to bring in newspapers, you can contact your local newspaper. Many publishers have specific programs for schools where copies of newspapers can be purchased at a reduced rate. Find an empty counter space and stack them in specific sections. For example, in one pile put sports, in another pile put want ads, etc.

Scavenger Hunts

Scavenger Hunts are random ten-item lists. No two students will have the same answers on their sheets upon completion of this activity. The lists are arranged from easy to difficult. Scavenger Hunt #1 is the easiest list. Scavenger Hunt #40 is the most difficult.

For this activity you may want to divide the class into groups. Have each group go to the newspaper counter and take a section from each pile. Give the groups a copy of work sheet page 131 to put their answers on. Each group will also need scissors and glue. Choose one of the ten-item Scavenger Hunt instructional sheets (pages 8–27) that is most appropriate for your grade level. You may want to set a timer for this activity, but it is not necessary. Give each group a copy of one of the Scavenger Hunt work sheets and begin. Students may use any section of the newspaper to find possible solutions. Allow students to use maps or other reference materials as needed.

Scavenger Games and Activities

Newspaper Scavenger Hunt Work Sheet

1. lake	2. computer
3. monkey	4. Montana
5. BEEN	6. Libby
7. Apple	8. water
9. Red Cherry	10. 50

© Teacher Created Materials, Inc.   131   #2353 Newspaper Scavenger Hunts

You will have to judge as to whether or not students find appropriate responses. Have students justify their answers if there are doubts. For example, the list item says *something that you eat for lunch*. Assume that a group of students glued the word "egg" on their answer sheet. You might respond by telling them that an egg is a breakfast food. If one student tells you that she had an egg salad sandwich for lunch, the group should be given credit for their response! Interactions like these are not uncommon. Allow students to use words or pictures from the newspaper, especially when the list item is followed by *word* or *picture*.

Content Hunts

Content Hunts are intended for use in a variety of curricular areas and themes. Look through the headings of the Content Hunts so that you are able to plan when you will use them during a particular area of study. Again, you may want to divide the class into groups or use the Content Hunts as a form of evaluation.

Give students a copy of the work sheet on page 131 to glue their answers on. Use the same directions as described above for the Scavenger Hunts.

Introduction *(cont.)*

Story Hunts

Story Hunts are paragraphs written to elicit humorous responses from students. Make copies of one page from the Story Hunts section on pages 56–65 and give to each student after they have collected their newspapers, scissors, and glue. Students will find words in the newspapers that fit into each of the ten blanks. Upon completion of the activity, have students read their paragraphs to the rest of the class. You may first want to check them to make sure of subject-verb agreement, etc.

Letter Hunts

Letter Hunts challenge students to search for appropriate letters to complete each clue. Possible answers are listed on page 138. Find a grade-appropriate Letter Hunt on pages 66–72 and give to each student or group. Students will cut letters from their newspapers to glue on each blank so that the words they create match the preceding clues. Encourage students to use easy-to-read letters from headlines or a bold typeset.

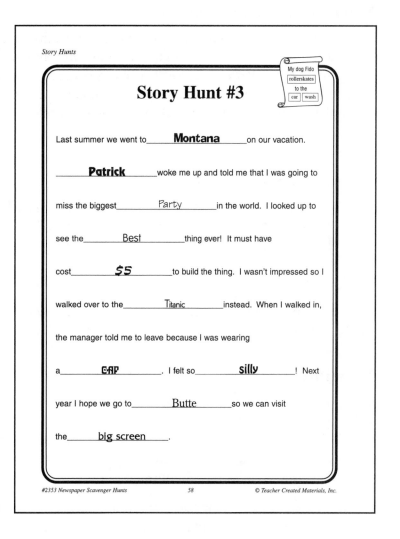

Book Hunts

Listed in the Table of Contents are twenty novels. For each book title there are three activities which include Vocabulary Hunts, Novel Hunts, and Style Hunts. You may want to review the activities in this section before you assign a novel to the class.

Vocabulary Hunts

Vocabulary Hunts are to be used as students read the novels. For each novel there are six hidden vocabulary words throughout the book. Listed on each Vocabulary Hunt work sheet are six clues and the approximate locations of the hidden words. As students read the novel they will find vocabulary words that match the clues. For more advanced readers, simply photocopy the appropriate work sheet and explain it to the students whom you assign to that particular novel. For other readers you may want to specify exact pages. There may be more than one possible answer depending on the word clues. Before assigning Vocabulary Hunts, you may want to explain to the students that the forms of the answers may vary from the clues. For example, a clue may say *to move without direction*, but the word in the book may say *wandering* instead of the word *wander*. Look at the answer key beginning on page 140 for solutions.

Introduction *(cont.)*

Novel Hunts

Novel Hunts are to be used in the same manner as Scavenger Hunts. Upon completion of a novel, give each student a copy of the Novel Hunt instructional sheet for that book title (pages 74–112) and a copy of the Novel Hunt Work Sheet for that title on page 131 to glue their responses on. Students will use the newspaper to find items pertinent to the novel they have read. Possible solutions are listed in the answer key beginning on page 140. Allow students to use their novels as a reference.

Style Hunts

Style Hunts will increase student awareness to various writing styles of children's authors. Students will use the novel to find interesting writing techniques including similes, metaphors, etc. Follow individual directions for each Style Hunt activity as each has a different focus. Possible answers are listed in the answer key beginning on page 140.

Scavenger Games and Activities

Scavenger Games and Activities are a variety of puzzles, art projects, and games. Some of these you will be able to incorporate into your curriculum. Follow individual directions for each game or activity.

Preparation

Since Scavenger Hunts, Novel Hunts, Letter Hunts, and Content Hunts are solely instructional pages, you may want to reproduce these pages onto cardstock and laminate. This will allow the sheets to last for several years. The laminated instructional pages can be hole-punched and kept in a three-ring binder for easy access. Hole-punch and file work sheets behind the corresponding instructional work sheets and copy them as they are needed.

You may want to photocopy the Scavenger Hunts, Content Hunts, Letter Hunts, and Novel Hunts. Laminate the copies and cut them in half for storage in a large index-card holder.

These activities involve intense teacher-student interaction. They are not designed to be low-maintenance seatwork for students!

Suggestions on How to Use This Book

Offer rewards for groups or individuals who finish early and are able to display good quality work when using Scavenger Hunts, Content Hunts, Novel Hunts, and Letter Hunts.

Distribute copies of work sheets facedown. Only after you say "GO" should students turn them over to begin. This ensures that no group or individual will have an unfair advantage.

Inform students at the outset of the activities that they may not come to the teacher until they have all ten of their responses glued to the work sheet on page 131 or to the specific Letter Hunt sheet (pages 66–72). At this point check all the responses at once. If you feel that one or more of the answers is inappropriate, allow students to try to correct their errors before another group finishes.

For group activities, you may want to have the students write their initials in the boxes after cutting and pasting their words and pictures on the work sheet on page 131 for Scavenger, Content, and Book Hunt activities. This method of labeling their work encourages fairness and teamwork.

Extension Activities

1. Make spelling lists from words that students find in the newspaper. Include words that are found when using Scavenger Hunt activities.

2. Graph the results of a Scavenger Hunt activity after students have completed a Scavenger Hunt, Content Hunt, or Novel Hunt. Write the items from the list on the board and ask volunteers to record their answers as data. Have members of your class organize the data into a bar graph.

3. Start a collection of magazines in your classroom. Apply many of the Scavenger Hunt activities to magazines and other periodicals.

4. Use any of the topics from the Scavenger Hunts as the basis for research activities. Assign reports or research papers to students who find their areas of interest in one of the activities in this book.

5. Use the Content Hunts section as an enjoyable form of evaluation. For example, if you have recently completed a unit on adverbs, give students the Adverb Hunt work sheet as their final exam.

6. Schedule a field trip to your local newspaper publisher. Most newspapers will accommodate your class. See how a newspaper is produced from the news reporting to the final publishing.

7. Have students use various sections of the newspaper to create their own word games.

8. Have students find additional facts on any of the Scavenger Hunt topics by using the Internet.

9. Students can make their own crossword puzzles. Provide them with copies of the Letter Hunt section to use as their clues.

10. Assign a Scavenger Hunt activity and allow students to use only pictures or cartoon drawings for their responses.

11. Write your own Scavenger Hunt if you are studying a specific content area. Use the work sheet on page 118 to organize your list.

12. Use words from Vocabulary Hunts as spelling words after you have finished a class novel. Also have students use the words in paragraphs or in other language activities.

Scavenger Hunt #1

Find the following:

1. a word with the /*sh*/ sound
2. the word "and"
3. a proper noun
4. a capital **D**
5. the name of a sports team

6. any headline
7. the number two
8. a picture of a bicycle
9. something you ride in
10. a picture with more than two people in it

Scavenger Hunt #2

Find the following:

1. something that is blue
2. something that holds liquids
3. the name of a state
4. a word that rhymes with bat
5. something that weighs more than you

6. something you drive
7. the first name of a girl
8. a place you could hide
9. something edible
10. what five + three equals

Scavenger Hunt #3

Find the following:

1. something that bounces
2. a day of the week
3. a word with a long **a** sound
4. something for sale
5. part of a crossword puzzle

6. a house
7. somewhere warm
8. what 10 + 25 equals
9. something you can wear
10. a question mark

Scavenger Hunt #4

Find the following:

1. the score of a game
2. any country
3. a person who works outdoors
4. something that can carry water
5. a weather prediction

6. a picture with a car in it
7. something an artist drew
8. the word "page"
9. a town or city in this state
10. a number between five and ten

Scavenger Hunt #5

Find the following:

1. an item that will fit in a truck

2. the name of a newspaper

3. this stretches

4. headline of a sports article

5. a word that describes the weather

6. a noun

7. a wild animal (word or picture)

8. a number that has three digits

9. something brown

10. a picture of a hat

Scavenger Hunt #6

Find the following:

1. a place more than 200 miles from here

2. something that is cold

3. words from a byline

4. a pet (word or picture)

5. a word that has the /ou/ sound

6. a picture of something you eat

7. a puzzle of any kind

8. an odd number

9. something you throw

10. this could be put on a hamburger

Scavenger Hunt #7

Find the following:

1. a state with mountains

2. something you use in art class

3. any amount of money

4. the word "work"

5. a person who attends college

6. a two-syllable word

7. a picture of a tire

8. something that juice is made from

9. a number that has two of the same digits in it

10. a word that ends with the letter **g**

Scavenger Hunt #8

Find the following:

1. a cold place

2. a picture that shows a garage or a shop

3. what a horse eats

4. something that will rust

5. something that you write with

6. a number with a five in the tens place

7. something inflammable

8. the word "been"

9. a word shown in all capital letters

10. somewhere you can swim

Scavenger Hunt #9

Find the following:

1. a word with an **x** in it

2. a picture of an occupied vehicle

3. the word "every"

4. any color (word only)

5. any place in Canada

6. the name of a movie

7. a verb

8. a word that has an -**er** ending

9. something you use to make cookies with

10. a phone number with two fives in it

Scavenger Hunt #10

Find the following:

1. a state that borders the Atlantic Ocean

2. the word "editor"

3. any place that is to the south of here

4. a picture with a man and a woman in it

5. a preposition

6. a word that has five syllables

7. any bird (word or picture)

8. sum of the digits of this number equals eight

9. a shoe company

10. a person who rescues others

Scavenger Hunt #11

Find the following:

1. a number greater than 50,000

2. a conjunction

3. the temperature in Los Angeles

4. a classified ad advertising a used truck

5. a city within 100 miles of here

6. a vehicle other than a car

7. a sentence with a compound subject

8. something you cook

9. any animal (word or picture)

10. the name of a plant

Scavenger Hunt #12

Find the following:

1. a person's face with glasses

2. the name of a professional football team

3. the word "because"

4. a letter from someone to the newspaper

5. a number smaller than one

6. a proper noun

7. an element

8. a man named Bill or William (word or picture)

9. the temperature in New York City

10. something you would use on your hair

Scavenger Hunt #13

Find the following:

1. the word "football"

2. a map of a state in the U.S. (picture)

3. either the word "percent" or its symbol

4. the price of a used snowmobile or motorcycle

5. a picture of a baby

6. any fraction (example, ½ or one half

7. a town north of here

8. a state east of the Mississippi River

9. a number between 350–400

10. an interrogative sentence

Scavenger Hunt #14

Find the following:

1. a city in another country

2. something you put on a pizza

3. an adjective

4. the name "Jim" or "James"

5. an abbreviation of a state

6. a city or town west of here

7. your age plus ten

8. a motorcycle (word or picture)

9. an exclamation mark

10. the name of a river

Scavenger Hunt #15

Find the following:

1. a number written out

2. any map (picture)

3. the name of a wild animal

4. a city south of here

5. a capital city in the United States

6. a picture with at least five people in it

7. the name of a continent

8. the price of any plant

9. a main verb and its helper

10. something you would put in a car

Scavenger Hunt #16

Find the following:

1. an adverb

2. a country in South America (word or picture)

3. a picture of someone's shoes

4. a professional basketball team

5. the word "snow"

6. the name of a tree or any plant

7. any kind of tool (word or picture)

8. a city with a temperature over 65° F (18° C)

9. a comic caption with the word "if" or "but" in it

10. a headline with a person's name in it

Scavenger Hunt #17

Find the following:

1. an ad selling something that you would use outside

2. the word "fall"

3. any circle

4. the name of any river or creek

5. the name of any animal

6. a pronoun

7. the name of a person from a different country

8. a horoscope

9. a number between 110 and 200

10. any type of ball from the sports pages

Scavenger Hunt #18

Find the following:

1. any drug or medicine

2. the word "people"

3. a state capital other than your own

4. any amount of money including the $ symbol

5. the temperature in any Texas city

6. the score from any athletic event

7. a domesticated animal (word or picture)

8. the name of two states other than your own

9. the name of a lake

10. a picture of a girl from the comics

Scavenger Hunt #19

Find the following:

1. a holiday

2. the word "number"

3. a post office box number

4. a common noun

5. something you would put in a car

6. a city with a population of over one million people

7. a three-syllable word

8. a four-door car

9. something that tells time (word or picture)

10. a whole number less than four

Scavenger Hunt #20

Find the following:

1. the name of any color

2. the word "from"

3. something that has an odor

4. a sentence that is quoted from someone

5. a picture of someone smiling

6. something that flies in the sky (word or picture)

7. a place that is east of here

8. a coin (word or picture)

9. a picture taken outside

10. a number that equals your age

Scavenger Hunt #21

Find the following:

1. the word "water"

2. a school subject

3. any type of plant (word or picture)

4. something you clean with

5. something worth more than $10,000

6. any body of water

7. a picture of a car or truck

8. a street address

9. a police officer (picture)

10. a state on the East Coast

Scavenger Hunt #22

Find the following:

1. the word "computer"

2. a state on the West Coast

3. the name of one of your classmates

4. an electrical conductor

5. either Alaska or Hawaii (word or picture)

6. any rectangle

7. a job advertisement

8. a possessive noun

9. any acronym: example, NASA

10. any place that is northeast of here

Scavenger Hunt #23

Find the following:

1. any country or geographic feature in Africa

2. the word "land"

3. something you would use in the kitchen

4. a plural noun

5. any star

6. a synonym for big

7. a **W** that is capitalized

8. something that is free

9. a compound word

10. anything made of metal (word or picture)

Scavenger Hunt #24

Find the following:

1. a summer month

2. any building (word or picture)

3. the word "new"

4. a picture of something made from wood

5. a wedding cake decoration (word or picture)

6. any place in Florida

7. something you would drink (word or picture)

8. an antonym for the word "hot"

9. a word that has the /qu/ sound in it

10. a number between 800–1000

Scavenger Hunt #25

Find the following:

1. any vitamin or drug

2. the word "before"

3. someone in trouble with the law

4. a food advertisement

5. a country north of the equator

6. a word that has the /wh/ sound in it

7. a schedule of any kind

8. a picture of someone's thumb

9. an adverb

10. the number 65

Scavenger Hunt #26

Find the following:

1. a town or city in Pennsylvania

2. the word "room"

3. something you put on tacos (word or picture)

4. any phone number

5. a caption in a comic strip

6. something checkered

7. a picture taken indoors

8. a county in your state

9. something you use at school

10. the number before 60

Scavenger Hunt #27

Find the following:

1. any instrument

2. the word "sale"

3. the price of this newspaper

4. a weather report (word or picture)

5. an animal seen at a zoo

6. land or a house for sale

7. any product other than a car or truck

8. a number divisible by eight

9. an actor or actress

10. any form of exercise

Scavenger Hunt #28

Find the following:

1. a picture of a person younger than you

2. the word "said"

3. a multiple of six

4. any individual sport

5. a cartoon with an animal in it

6. an old building

7. a picture with only one person in it

8. something that makes noise

9. an animal that might be hunted

10. any product that is on sale

Scavenger Hunt #29

Find the following:

1. a precious metal

2. something that is flammable

3. a picture of someone smiling

4. the word "salvage"

5. a breakfast food

6. a car at least 12 years old in the want ads

7. a road, highway, or street

8. something that plays music (word or picture)

9. an ordinal number

10. a state that borders Canada

Scavenger Hunt #30

Find the following:

1. any fall month

2. the word "police"

3. someplace you could sleep

4. a plural possessive noun

5. a city temperature above 70° F (21° C)

6. a country in Europe

7. any form of precipitation

8. someone who works in Washington, D.C.

9. any kind of meat

10. 10 percent of 40

Scavenger Hunt #31

Find the following:

1. a hoofed animal

2. any piece of jewelry (word or picture)

3. number of sides on a pentagon

4. a headline with six words

5. a prime number greater than 26

6. a store that sells parts

7. an item larger than your house

8. a city in the Eastern Hemisphere

9. a factor of 54

10. what a biologist studies

Scavenger Hunt #32

Find the following:

1. the first three square numbers

2. a country that is also an island

3. something used to make cement

4. a state south of the 45 degree parallel

5. a vertical line

6. you use this to sew with

7. a paragraph with three sentences in it

8. a multiple of 20

9. an invertebrate (word or picture)

10. what a gallon of water weighs

Scavenger Hunt #33

Find the following:

1. a state that starts with an **M**

2. a polygon

3. a win-loss record

4. any measurement

5. the atomic symbol for oxygen

6. a year prior to 1980

7. a word with a double consonant

8. a country above the 40-degree south parallel

9. a European country

10. the greatest common factor of 24 and 20

Scavenger Hunt #34

Find the following:

1. an adjective from a headline

2. a circle with a radius greater than one inch

3. a federal employee

4. a number greater than 100

5. a picture of parallel lines

6. an airplane for sale

7. a city east of the 80-degree west meridian

8. a picture of someone wearing a long-sleeved shirt

9. something you put a stamp on

10. any graph

Scavenger Hunt #35

Find the following:

1. a drawing of sun or clouds

2. a stringed instrument

3. a car that does not run

4. an animal not found in America

5. the least common multiple of six and eight

6. a professional team that has an omnivorous mascot

7. a body of water south of here

8. the words "Dow Jones"

9. a part from a motorcycle

10. a city's name that is at least two words

Scavenger Hunt #36

Find the following:

1. a statistic

2. a stock worth more than 20 dollars per share

3. an arrow

4. a city with at least three different vowels in its name

5. a business for sale

6. a rectangle with an area greater than seven inches

7. the name of a boat or a ship

8. any college sports team name

9. a horizontal line

10. one of the original 13 colonies

Scavenger Hunt #37

Find the following:

1. something orange

2. a nonconductor

3. a number greater than 50 that is divisible by 12

4. a rodeo animal

5. any organism

6. the atomic symbol for boron

7. an ethnic food

8. something that has seeds in it

9. a continent dissected by the 20-degree east meridian

10. something that is lacking during a drought

Scavenger Hunt #38

Find the following:

1. the first three cube numbers

2. a person who died recently

3. a food high in protein

4. the atomic symbol of an element in glucose

5. an ocean or sea dissected by the prime meridian

6. a language other than English

7. a four-syllable word

8. a peninsula (word or picture)

9. a semicolon

10. a hibernating animal

Scavenger Hunt #39

Find the following:

1. the square root of 441

2. a company logo

3. an international headline

4. a rational number

5. a simile or metaphor

6. a truck with a diesel engine (word or picture)

7. a reptile (word or picture)

8. the word "lawyer" or "judge"

9. a Rocky Mountain state

10. stock listing of a food company

Scavenger Hunt #40

Find the following:

1. an ungulate species

2. forms a wave from the electromagnetic spectrum

3. an isobar

4. an insect that flies

5. an organic product

6. ten percent of N + three = eight

7. stock listing of a petroleum producer

8. periodic chart symbol for potassium

9. first three Fibonacci numbers

10. a large city at 41 degrees north, 74 degrees west

Rhyme Hunt

Find as many rhyming words as possible for each item:

1. kind
2. glue
3. blow
4. range
5. school

6. way
7. best
8. see
9. many
10. kite

Rhyme Hunt

Find as many rhyming words as possible for each item:

1. heather
2. mad
3. tying
4. depend
5. might

6. rage
7. define
8. fry
9. ton
10. per

Synonym Hunt

Find as many synonyms as possible for each item:

1. strong

2. tired

3. incredible

4. saga

5. scurry

6. trip

7. neat

8. under

9. powerful

10. think

Synonym Hunt

Find as many synonyms as possible for each item:

1. preserve

2. scratch

3. necessary

4. tributary

5. partial

6. near

7. uncertain

8. plenty

9. thin

10. kind

Antonym Hunt

Find as many antonyms as possible for each item:

1. high

2. inside

3. give

4. stale

5. honest

6. healthy

7. cold

8. future

9. play

10. seldom

Antonym Hunt

Find as many antonyms as possible for each item:

1. found

2. interesting

3. release

4. carefully

5. friend

6. guard

7. intelligent

8. fix

9. flimsy

10. clean

Homophone Hunt

Find as many homophones as possible for each item:

1. coarse

2. pier

3. threw

4. red

5. hear

6. to

7. feet

8. towed

9. there

10. weigh

Homophone Hunt

Find as many homophones as possible for each item:

1. flour

2. fore

3. their

4. principle

5. flu

6. two

7. reed

8. suite

9. meet

10. beet

Suffix Hunt

Find as many words as possible that end with each suffix:

1. est

2. ed

3. ing

4. er

5. ity

6. ness

7. ment

8. ive

9. ist

10. able

Suffix Hunt

Find as many words as possible that end with each suffix:

1. ish

2. ous

3. ant

4. ic

5. or

6. ize

7. en

8. hood

9. es

10. tion

Prefix Hunt

Find as many words as possible that begin with each prefix:

1. pre

2. du

3. con

4. de

5. post

6. tri

7. semi

8. in

9. mid

10. un

Prefix Hunt

Find as many words as possible that begin with each prefix:

1. dis

2. non

3. im

4. fore

5. ex

6. re

7. pro

8. co

9. inter

10. com

Sentence Hunt

Find the following sentence types:

1. a sentence that has a compound predicate

2. a sentence that has ten words in it

3. a declarative sentence

4. a sentence that has an interjection in it

5. an exclamatory sentence

6. a sentence that has five words in it

7. an interrogative sentence

8. a sentence that mentions at least two people

9. an imperative sentence

10. a sentence with two subjects

Abbreviation Hunt

Find words for the following abbreviations:

1. hr.

2. qt.

3. apt.

4. ave.

5. oz.

6. yr.

7. lb.

8. doz.

9. co.

10. wt.

Word Hunt

Find the following words:

1. a word that shows joy

2. a word that shows sorrow

3. a word that shows regret

4. a word that shows danger

5. a word that shows victory

6. a word that shows emotion

7. a word that shows boredom

8. a word that shows stress

9. a word that shows freedom

10. a word that shows cunning

Sound Hunt

Find words with the following sounds:

1. a word with the /j/ sound

2. a word with the /ch/ sound

3. a word with the long **e** sound

4. a word with the long **a** sound

5. a word with the /oi/ sound

6. a word with the short **i** sound

7. a word with the /k/ sound

8. a word with the short **o** sound

9. a word with the /sh/ sound

10. a word with the /ou/ sound

Noun Hunt

Find the following nouns:

1. a noun you can drink

2. a plural noun

3. a noun that names an athlete

4. a noun that is an animal

5. a noun that floats

6. a possessive noun

7. a plural noun ending with **ies**

8. a noun with more than seven letters in it

9. a plural noun not ending in **s**

10. a noun from the headlines

Common and Proper Nouns Hunt

Find the following common or proper nouns:

1. a proper noun that is a person

2. a common noun that is a place

3. a sentence that has a common and a proper noun

4. a proper noun from the sports page

5. a singular common noun

6. a proper noun you can eat

7. a plural proper noun

8. a proper noun that is a place (word or picture)

9. a common noun you can drive

10. a common noun that is a thing

Verb Hunt

Find the following verbs:

1. a verb that ends in -**ed**

2. an action verb

3. a verb phrase with three words in it

4. a verb from the headlines

5. a verb in the present tense

6. a verb from the weather page

7. a verb in the past tense

8. a verb phrase with two words in it

9. a verb that is a contraction

10. a verb in the future tense

Verb Hunt

Find verbs or verb phrases that fit into the following sentences:

1. He was_____about the weather.

2. They_____her over the fence.

3. If he_____, we will see him.

4. Her head_____but she is okay.

5. I did not_____that movie.

6. The tiny car_____to miss the truck.

7. Horses_____when the weather turns cold.

8. The tornado_____through our yard.

9. His sense of humor _____since the wreck.

10. The story_____a happy ending.

Adjective Hunt

Find the following adjectives and the nouns they describe:

1. an adjective that tells how many

2. an adjective that describes a car

3. an adjective that describes the weather

4. an adjective that describes the height of something

5. an adjective that is a color

6. a noun that is described by two or more adjectives

7. an adjective that ends in -**est**

8. an adjective that describes an athlete

9. a proper adjective

10 an adjective from the comics

Adjective Hunt

Find adjectives that modify the following nouns:

1. weather

2. truck

3. teacher

4. boys

5. animal

6. school

7. shirt

8. storm

9. road

10. player

Adverb Hunt

Find the following adverbs and the verbs they modify:

1. an adverb that ends in **-ly**

2. an adverb that ends in **-est**

3. an adverb that ends in **-er**

4. an adverb that tells **how**

5. an adverb that tells **when**

6. an adverb that tells **where**

7. an adverb that has "most" before it

8. an adverb that has "more" before it

9. an adverb that comes before the verb

10. an adverb that comes after the verb

Adverb Hunt

Find adverbs to modify each of the following verbs:

1. laughed

2. flew

3. surprised

4. yelled

5. walked

6. stood

7. followed

8. played

9. sang

10. fell

Preposition Hunt

Find prepositions that fit in the following phrases:

1. sea level
2. the window
3. a doubt
4. the river
5. the corner

6. the barn
7. the hill
8. tomorrow
9. the counter
10. 9:30 A.M.

Object of the Preposition Hunt

Find objects for the following prepositions:

1. above the
2. except for
3. during the
4. near the
5. outside the

6. until
7. through the
8. inside the
9. without her
10. off

Pronoun Hunt

Find pronouns that correctly fit into the sentences.

1. ____and I went to the movie.

2. The bus left without Jim and____.

3. ____children want more recess time!

4. The award was won by____.

5. ____has a red stripe on it.

6. ____lived on Mars for one year.

7. I think____have done a great job.

8. Bill visited Marie and____.

9. ____tour guide was funny.

10. Leslie and Ashley learned____very quickly.

Conjunction Hunt

Find conjunctions that fit into the blanks below.

1. Deer can run____ jump well.

2. He wants either juice____milk.

3. Their heads are large,____ their tails are short.

4. We should go to the park____ join them.

5. The others liked the corn,____I liked the beans.

6. They build their nests in trees____in shrubs.

7. Fish____insects move faster than we think.

8. The weather is bad,____we have enough to do inside.

9. We can eat here____go outside.

10. Davey____Michael are best friends.

Punctuation Hunt

Cut and glue the appropriate punctuation marks in the sentences below.

1. We asked the clerk for the catalog

2. Marie asked Did you find the watch yet?

3. Where is the bus going to stop first

4. Oh my goodness The picture turned out horribly

5. Where is the best place to eat? asked Margie.

6. I do not understand why he wants us to follow him

7. What a tremendous effort he displayed

8. I think Benedict Arnold was a traitor

9. My address is PO Box 456

10. The St. Louis Blues are my favorite hockey team

Capital Letter Hunt

Cut and glue the correct capital letters over the letter mistakes in the sentences below.

1. Many professional players live in Washington, d.c.

2. the mississippi river is among the largest in america.

3. I have always admired mr. johnson for his courage.

4. The best houses are on Jones creek.

5. He lives on the north side of sutton street.

6. sergeant MacDonald lives in the Smith barracks.

7. The capital of wyoming is cheyenne.

8. i.b.m. makes excellent computer systems.

9. Our barn is on ryeburg road.

10. the tree by the fence is a memorial to Miss coughlin.

42

Social Studies Hunt

Find the following:

1. the first U.S. president, first or last name

2. a state in the Dust Bowl region

3. any member of Congress

4. any imported product

5. a slave state

6. another name for a duty

7. any of the original colonies

8. minimum age of a voter

9. the first name of any U.S. president

10. a product that is exported

Social Studies Hunt

Find the following:

1. a natural resource

2. something pioneers used to build cabins

3. a state where the Plains Indians lived

4. something you can recycle

5. a place with a dry climate

6. something that makes pollution

7. a mineral

8. a form of transportation other than a car or truck

9. a national holiday

10. a symbol of America

Geography Hunt

Find the following:

1. a city in your state

2. any kind of park

3. any country

4. a state with a desert in it

5. a city on a coast

6. any cardinal direction

7. a state south of Iowa

8. a place on a different continent

9. a state that grows fruit

10. the name of any creek or river

Geography Hunt

Find the following:

1. a continent mostly in the Southern Hemisphere

2. a town or city within 1,000 miles of the North Pole

3. a city near the Great Lakes

4. a strait

5. any place in the Eastern Hemisphere

6. a state that borders Colorado

7. a city with an elevation of over 3,000 feet

8. a city in Europe

9. a river or lake in a foreign country

10. a city name with Spanish origins

City Nickname Hunt

Find the cities that have the following nicknames:

1. The City of Lights

2. The City of Brotherly Love

3. The Windy City

4. The Alamo City

5. The Bay City

6. The Mile High City

7. The City of Angels

8. The Emerald City

9. The Big D

10. The Big Apple

Country Hunt

Find the country for each capital listed below:

1. Moscow

2. Nairobi

3. Madrid

4. Brasilia

5. Paris

6. Oslo

7. Berlin

8. New Delhi

9. Canberra

10. Tokyo

State Nickname Hunt

Find states for the following nicknames:

1. The Bluegrass State

2. The Hawkeye State

3. The Sunshine State

4. The Sooner State

5. The Lone Star State

6. The Silver State

7. The Keystone State

8. The Gem State

9. The Garden State

10. The Wolverine State

State Nickname Hunt

Find states for the following nicknames:

1. The Beehive State

2. The Aloha State

3. The First State

4. The Volunteer State

5. Land of Lincoln

6. The Empire State

7. The Tar Heel State

8. The Treasure State

9. The Golden State

10. The Badger State

State/Capital Hunt

Find the state or capital of the following:

1. Bismarck
2. Salem
3. Rhode Island
4. Richmond
5. Albany

6. Dover
7. Nebraska
8. St. Paul
9. Wyoming
10. Frankfort

State/Capital Hunt

Find the state or capital of the following:

1. Idaho
2. Indiana
3. Montpelier
4. Ohio
5. Colorado

6. Baton Rouge
7. Augusta
8. Mississippi
9. Raleigh
10. Olympia

Science Hunt

Find the following:

1. any gaseous element

2. an insulator

3. an example of a mixture

4. a buoyant object

5. something attracted by a magnet

6. the word "humidity"

7. a good conductor

8. something that reduces friction

9. atomic number of gold

10. produces static electricity

Biology Hunt

Find the following:

1. a cold-blooded animal

2. a whale's habitat

3. a high-fiber food

4. elements in soil

5. a food chain producer

6. a human body mineral

7. the letters **ph**

8. any chromosome symbol

9. a warm-blooded animal

10. an animal that has gills

Math Hunt

Find the following:

1. the greatest common divisor of 12 and 48

2. the square root of 81

3. the numbers in the prime factorization of 20

4. the number 63 rounded to the nearest tens place

5. a number with a five in the hundreds place

6. a three-digit number divisible by three

7. a prime number greater than 30

8. a negative integer

9. the least common multiple of 9 and 15

10. 25 percent of 800

Geometry Hunt

Find the following:

1. a rectangle

2. a regular polygon

3. a trapezoid

4. an obtuse angle

5. any circle

6. a cylinder

7. a square

8. two congruent figures

9. two similar figures

10. any triangle

Astronomy Hunt

Find the following:

1. the name of a star other than our sun

2. any planet other than Earth

3. the word "universe"

4. a satellite

5. the sun

6. a galaxy

7. a movie or television show about space

8. the name of a comet

9. a space vehicle

10. a product named after something in space

Plant Hunt

Find the following:

1. a picture of a coniferous tree

2. a cone-bearing tree (word or picture)

3. a picture of any plant other than a tree

4. a fruit producer

5. a deciduous tree (word or picture)

6. a cash crop

7. a weed

8. the name of a forest

9. a toxic plant

10. something a plant needs for survival

Animal Hunt

Find words or pictures for the following:

1. a bovine species

2. an ungulate species

3. a migratory animal

4. an omnivorous animal

5. an amphibian

6. an endangered species

7. an herbivore

8. a raptor

9. a game animal

10. a carnivore

Sports Hunt

Use the sports pages to find the following:

1. a picture with more than one athlete in it

2. an injured person

3. an individual sport

4. a schedule of sporting events

5. a quote from an athlete

6. a sport played outdoors

7. a television network that covers sports

8. a won-loss record

9. a sporting event that was played near your hometown

10. the last name of a high school athlete

Advertisement Hunt

Use the classified section to find the following:

1. something that is lost

2. something that is new

3. the word "finance"

4. a kitchen appliance for sale

5. an apartment for rent

6. something that is free

7. a non-wheeled item for sale

8. someone who will clean or fix something

9. something for sale that you could use in your garden

10. any type of trailer for sale

Weather Hunt

Use the weather page to find the following:

1. what time the sun will rise

2. the word "mild"

3. a record high temperature

4. the symbol for high pressure

5. the temperature of a city in Alaska

6. a city that has clouds over it

7. the time of the sunset

8. a record low temperature

9. a forecast

10. a symbol for a form of precipitation

Literary Hunt

Find examples of these literary terms in the newspaper:

1. personification

2. hyperbole

3. a metaphor

4. a simile

5. onomatopoeia

6. alliteration

7. an author of a novel

8. an idiom

9. consonance

10. any genre

Newspaper Hunt

Find examples of the following newspaper terms:

1. a caption

2. a headline

3. a byline

4. a masthead

5. an obituary

6. an Associated Press story

7. a dateline

8. a flag or a nameplate

9. a lead paragraph

10. a story with a jump

Valentine's Day Hunt

Find words or pictures for the following items:

1. the word "saint"

2. chocolate

3. a heart

4. the word "your"

5. flowers

6. a card

7. Cupid

8. the color red

9. an arrow

10. a Valentine's wish to someone

St. Patrick's Day Hunt

Find words or pictures for the following items:

1. an Irish flag

2. a leprechaun

3. a pot of gold

4. a shamrock

5. cabbage

6. the color green

7. a parade

8. the word "lucky"

9. a four-leaf clover

10. corned beef

Christmas Hunt

Find words or pictures for the following items:

1. a Christmas tree

2. Santa

3. the word "merry"

4. a present

5. stockings

6. a wreath

7. a snowflake

8. reindeer

9. an ornament

10. a turkey

Easter Hunt

Find words or pictures for the following items:

1. a bunny

2. something smaller than an egg

3. the name of a church

4. any type of candy

5. the word "April"

6. a basket

7. something that reminds you of spring

8. eggs

9. a raindrop

10. a ham or a turkey

Story Hunt #1

Today we had a great time!_____and I went to the

park. We found a_____by the bench to play with.

It was_____and_____.

_____put it in the pond. Then we knew we were in

big trouble because_____saw us and came running

toward us. He told us that we should_____before

the mayor saw this mess. We took his advice and started for

_____. I hope that

_____doesn't find out. If that happens I will

be_____for the rest of my life!

Story Hunt #2

My dog Fido rollerskates to the car wash

Have you ever tried to make a_____? It's really not

as hard as it seems. First you must be in a_____.

And if there are any_____nearby, you must remove

them. Start by mixing _____ and

_____ together. Then pour into a

large_____. Very carefully, stir in the magic potion

made from_____. Before you drink it, make sure

that you are wearing a_____. If you start

turning_____, you need to see

a_____immediately!

Story Hunt #3

Last summer we went to_____on our vacation.

_____woke me up and told me that I was going to

miss the biggest_____in the world. I looked up to

see the_____thing ever! It must have cost

_____to build the thing. I wasn't impressed, so I

walked over to the_____instead. When I walked in,

the manager told me to leave because I was wearing a

_____. I felt so_____! Next

year I hope we go to_____so we can visit

the_____.

Story Hunt #4

I like being outdoors because you always see_____

and smell the_____.

The_____flows down the stream. The trees in the

forest are_____.   Sometimes

_____and I go for walks in the evening. When it

starts to get dark, you can look up in the sky and see

_____. When the sun goes down, it

starts to get_____, and we start heading for

the_____. We turn on our

_____to find our way back. Then we relax and go

to_____.

Story Hunt #5

Cowboy Bob is a modern-day_____cowboy.

Instead of a horse, he uses a_____. He goes to

the_____to round up his

_____. Bob doesn't sit around the campfire and

sing songs like the old cowboys. He uses

a_____to keep him warm and listens

to_____music. In the_____he

rides a wild horse. If he gets bucked off, everyone tells him

to_____. Then Bob goes home and

eats_____for dinner and thinks about

Story Hunt #6

_____trucks always break down. Yesterday on our

way to the_____, we stalled out.

_____looked under the hood and said that

the_____was missing. We called

_____to come and tow us in. He didn't break

down, but on the way to the shop a_____fell out

and hit the_____. _____saw

it happen and told us to_____the next time this

happened. We said, "This wouldn't happen again because we were

going to_____!"

Story Hunt #7

It was the best_____ I have ever played.

_____is a hard game, but when you score points it

seems easy. Every time_____threw me the ball, I

went into a_____zone.

_____, our new coach, told me that I would

start_____for the rest of the year.

_____also played a great game. But in the third

quarter he broke his_____. Now our chances of

making it to the tournament in_____are not very

good. We play our old rival tomorrow. If we win, we are going

to_____for dinner!

Story Hunt #8

Today I saw_____at the county fair.

_____was with him so I didn't say anything to him.

He won a_____when he broke ten

_____with one throw. Then they walked over to the

ride. We were going to follow them on the _____,

but_____said she got sick last year when the

ride_____. I think she ate too much. We saw them

again in the parade waving their_____. They were

riding_____, and they looked

_____!

Story Hunts

Story Hunt #9

My dad used to be a_____. But he thought he

could make more money fixing_____. I'm going to

college in five years. I want to be a_____because I

like working with_____. My dad should have been

a_____, but his feet are too

_____. Mom likes her job, but working

for_____would be fun. She really wanted

to_____for her career. Instead, she had the

opportunity to_____at the circus. We all have had

one aspiration in common; we'd like to_____in a

marching band.

Story Hunt #10

My dog Fido
rollerskates
to the
car wash

The magic hat makes you feel_____. I think

the_____on top is the secret. I found it at

the_____. I think it belonged to an old

_____. The tag inside the hat had the

number_____on it. When Rachel put it on,

she started to_____. We had to

pour_____on her. She had a

_____look in her eye. The magic hat

is_____. Now I keep the hat at home so that no

one will_____.

Letter Hunt #1

Use letters from the newspaper to solve the following:

1. a cap
   ___ ___ t

2. young cat
   ___ i ___ t ___ ___

3. a lawn
   g ___ a ___ s

4. a window
   ___ l ___ s ___

5. makes you warm
   s ___ ___

6. big boat
   s ___ ___ p

7. opposite of in
   ___ u ___

8. coin
   p ___ ___ n ___

9. insect
   f ___ ___

10. laugh
    g ___ g ___ ___ e

Letter Hunt #2

Use letters from the newspaper to solve the following:

1. a tailless primate
   ___ p ___

2. opposite of fat
   ___ k ___ n ___ ___

3. helps a kite
   w ___ n ___

4. kings wear a
   ___ r ___ w ___

5. chopping tool
   ___ x ___

6. above the neck
   ___ e ___ d

7. evening meal
   ___ ___ p ___ e ___

8. fruit
   o ___ a ___ ___ e

9. tardy
   ___ ___ ___ e

10. the sound a sheep makes
    ___ a ___

Letter Hunt #3

Use letters from the newspaper to solve the following:

1. grows on old bread

    m ___ l ___

2. helps you sleep

    p ___ ___ l ___ w

3. there's no place like

    ___ o ___ e

4. opposite of no

    ___ e ___

5. male cat

    ___ ___ m

6. grin

    ___ m i ___ e

7. young deer

    f ___ ___ n

8. has five fingers

    ___ a ___ d

9. hits a golf ball

    ___ l ___ b

10. a show with clowns

    c ___ r ___ ___ s

Letter Hunt #4

Use letters from the newspaper to solve the following:

1. one less than four

    ___ h ___ ___ e

2. he is, you

    ___ r ___

3. Eskimo home

    ___ g ___ ___ o

4. cuts paper

    s ___ i ___ ___ o ___ s

5. young cow

    ___ a l ___

6. shoots an arrow

    ___ o ___

7. catches fish

    ___ e ___

8. strange

    ___ d ___

9. a tree

    p ___ ___ e

10. North

    P ___ ___ e

Letter Hunt #5

Use letters from the newspaper to solve the following:

1. not wide

   n ___ ___ r ___ ___

2. big bird

   s ___ a ___

3. use to row

   o ___ r

4. not many

   ___ ___ w

5. narrow boat

   ___ a ___ ___ e

6. racquet sport

   ___ e ___ n ___ s

7. between streets

   ___ ___ l ___ y

8. not often

   ___ a ___ e ___ y

9. none

   ___ e ___ o

10. cabin type

    ___ o ___

Letter Hunt #6

Use letters from the newspaper to solve the following:

1. do at night

   ___ l ___ ___ p

2. place to eat

   ___ a ___ ___

3. write with

   ___ ___ n ___ i ___

4. opposite of loose

   ___ i ___ h ___

5. close

   n ___ ___ r

6. throw

   t ___ ___ s

7. measure with

   ___ u ___ e ___

8. by the ocean

   ___ h ___ r ___

9. car replica

   m ___ ___ e ___

10. alone

    s ___ l ___

68

Letter Hunt #7

Use letters from the newspaper to solve the following:

1. in a fireplace
   ___ ___ h

2. a playing card
   ___ c ___

3. stringed instrument
   ___ u ___ t ___ ___

4. not fancy
   ___ l ___ i ___

5. makes balloons fly
   h ___ l ___ ___ ___

6. put on burger
   ___ i ___ ___ l ___

7. summer month
   ___ ___ n ___

8. musical show
   ___ p ___ ___ a

9. type of bread
   ___ y ___

10. to lose weight
    d ___ ___ t

Letter Hunt #8

Use letters from the newspaper to solve the following:

1. moving snow
   a ___ ___ l ___ n ___ ___ e

2. dries you
   ___ o ___ e ___

3. mouth harp
   ___ a ___ m ___ ___ i ___ ___

4. plays music
   ___ a ___ i ___

5. opposite of sweet
   t ___ ___ t

6. punches
   ___ ___ x ___ s

7. gives light
   ___ a ___ p

8. bull's herd
   h ___ r ___ m

9. use when cold
   ___ l ___ v ___ s

10. one who arrests
    ___ h ___ ___ ___ f ___

Letter Hunt #9

Use letters from the newspaper to solve the following:

1. early town
   s ___ t ___ l ___ ___ e ___ t

2. cook
   r ___ ___ s ___

3. place to stay
   ___ n ___

4. bowling targets
   ___ i ___ ___

5. use at night
   ___ l ___ s ___ l ___ ___ h t

6. circus person
   ___ l ___ ___ n

7. gather
   c ___ ___ l ___ c ___

8. a pain
   b ___ t ___ e ___

9. not dull
   ___ h ___ ___ p

10. played from a horse
    ___ o ___ o

Letter Hunt #10

Use letters from the newspaper to solve the following:

1. to say one is sorry
   a ___ o ___ o ___ i ___ e

2. sweet
   ___ ___ g ___ r

3. town
   v ___ ___ l ___ g ___

4. farm alarm clock
   r ___ ___ s ___ ___ r

5. wonderful
   g ___ o ___ i ___ u ___

6. big bear
   ___ r ___ z ___ ___ y

7. coin
   ___ ___ a ___ ___ e ___

8. evening meal
   ___ i ___ n ___ r

9. facial hair
   m ___ s ___ a ___ h ___

10. protects consumers
    w ___ r ___ a ___ ___ y

Letter Hunt #11

Use letters from the newspaper to solve the following:

1. top secret
   c l ___ s ___ i ___ i e d

2. young horse
   ___ o ___ t

3. place to build
   ___ i ___ e

4. many uses
   v ___ ___ s ___ t ___ l ___

5. long lasting
   ___ u ___ a ___ l ___

6. what something holds
   ___ o ___ u ___ e

7. lose
   m ___ s ___ l ___ c ___

8. move
   r ___ l ___ ___ a ___ e

9. not rough
   s ___ ___ o ___ ___

10. liquids
    ___ l ___ i ___ s

Letter Hunt #12

Use letters from the newspaper to solve the following:

1. gripe
   c ___ ___ p ___ a ___ n

2. shooting star
   m ___ ___ e ___ ___

3. permit
   l ___ c ___ ___ s ___

4. epidemic
   ___ l ___ g ___ e

5. medium or middle in music
   m ___ z ___ o

6. quick
   h ___ s ___ y

7. death notice
   ___ b ___ ___ u ___ r ___

8. suggest
   ___ e n ___ i ___ n

9. after 11:59 P.M.
   m ___ d ___ ___ g ___ t

10. tools
    h ___ r ___ w ___ ___ e

Letter Hunt #13

Use letters from the newspaper to solve the following:

1. smoke vent
    c ___ i ___ ___ e ___

2. sacred song
    p ___ a ___ m

3. school helper
    ___ u ___ o ___

4. join
    u ___ i ___ e

5. tooth puller
    ___ e ___ ___ i ___ t

6. French servant
    v ___ l ___ t

7. uncooked
    ___ a ___

8. fancy clothes
    t ___ x ___ d ___

9. throw out
    e ___ ___ c ___

10. animal study
    ___ ___ o ___ o ___ y

Letter Hunt #14

Use letters from the newspaper to solve the following:

1. hardened
    p ___ t ___ ___ f ___ e ___

2. guard
    ___ r ___ t ___ ___ t

3. voyage
    ___ o ___ ___ n ___ y

4. rough character
    r ___ g ___ ___

5. check
    i ___ s ___ e ___ t

6. bus stop
    ___ e ___ o ___

7. pro
    e ___ p ___ ___ ___

8. push
    ___ h ___ ___ e

9. hole maker
    ___ r ___ l ___

10. enables one to taste
    ___ o ___ g ___ e

72

Vocabulary Hunt

Find the following vocabulary words when reading *From the Mixed-Up Files of Mrs. Basil E. Frankweiler* by E. L. Konigsburg.

Chapters 1–2 Clues   Find a synonym for the word "improper" that has a prefix and three syllables.

Word _____ page _____

Chapters 3–4 Clues   This word means "nothing inside." It has a suffix and three syllables.

Word _____ page _____

Chapter 5 Clues   The name of this soft cloth material contains four consonants and two syllables.

Word _____ page _____

Chapters 6–7 Clues   This word is a three-syllable adverb that means "very carefully."

Word _____ page _____

Chapter 8 Clues   Find a word that means "said again." It has a prefix and a suffix and three syllables.

Word _____ page _____

Chapters 9–10 Clues   This two-syllable word means "moved slowly." It has a suffix.

Word _____ page _____

Novel Hunt

Use the newspaper to find the following items from *From the Mixed-Up Files of Mrs. Basil E. Frankweiler* by E. L. Konigsburg.

1. purchase price of the statue

2. where Claudia and Jamie found money

3. Saxonberg's occupation

4. a street in New York City

5. setting of the story

6. an ingredient in *nouilles et fromage*

7. where the children hid in the museum

8. the name of the statue

9. Jamie's grade level

10. Michelangelo's home, city or country

Style Hunt

Look up the word *idiom* in the dictionary and write the definition in the space provided below.

idiom _____

_____

Find the idiom in Chapter One of *From the Mixed-Up Files of Mrs. Basil E. Frankweiler* by E. L. Konigsburg. Write this idiom in the space provided below.

an idiom from Chapter One _____

_____

Think of an idiom you have heard before and write it below.

_____

_____

Vocabulary Hunt

Find the following vocabulary words when reading *Tuck Everlasting* by Natalie Babbitt.

Chapters 1–4 Clues   Find a word that names a type of insect. The first letter of the word is silent, and it contains one syllable.

Word _____ page _____

Chapters 5–8 Clues   This three-syllable word means "moving without a set direction." It contains three vowels.

Word _____ page _____

Chapters 9–12 Clues   This word means "strange or odd." It has three syllables, and the last four letters describe an untruthful person.

Word _____ page _____

Chapters 13–16 Clues   Find a word that has the long **e** sound that means "within the law." It has two syllables.

Word _____ page _____

Chapters 17–20 Clues   This word names a partial amount. It has the /k/ sound and two syllables.

Word _____ page _____

Chapters 21–25 Clues   Find a word that means "nervous." More than half of the letters are vowels, and it contains two syllables.

Word _____ page _____

Novel Hunt

Use the newspaper to find items from *Tuck Everlasting* by Natalie Babbitt.

1. an animal from the story

2. the number of years since the Tucks drank the water

3. the word "jail"

4. a word that describes the weather in the story

5. a person from the book who did not drink the water

6. any story setting

7. the first name of a character from the story

8. physical condition of the constable

9. one of Tuck's breakfast foods

10. color of the man's suit

Style Hunt

Look up the word *analogy* in your dictionary and write the definition in the space provided below.

analogy _____

_____

Reread the prologue of the story *Tuck Everlasting* by Natalie Babbitt and find where an analogy is used. Write the analogy in the space provided below.

an analogy from the prologue _____

_____

Can you think of another analogy? Write your analogy below. _____

_____

Vocabulary Hunt

Find the following vocabulary words when reading *Call It Courage* by Armstrong Sperry.

Chapter 1 Clues   Find a word that describes a flow of water. It has a double consonant and two syllables.

Word _____ page _____

Chapter 2 Clues   This describes the furthest point you can see. The middle letter is an **i**, and the word contains three syllables.

Word _____ page _____

Chapter 3 Clues   This word means "something that belongs to someone." This word has six consonants and three syllables.

Word _____ page _____

Chapter 4 Clues   Find a one-syllable word that means "grabbed quickly." This word has the long **e** sound.

Word _____ page _____

Chapter 5 Clues   This word means "getting smaller." It has the long **a** sound and contains two syllables.

Word _____ page _____

Chapter 5 Clues   This word names persons who are chasing someone. This is a plural word that contains three syllables.

Word _____ page _____

Novel Hunt

Use a newspaper to find the following items from *Call It Courage* by Armstrong Sperry.

1. an animal Mafatu killed on the island

2. any setting of the story

3. what a kiwi is

4. stole from Mafatu's trap

5. type of boat used in the story (word or picture)

6. what Uri is

7. any weapon the natives used

8. Mafatu's biggest fear

9. a fruit mentioned in the story

10. directions of Mafatu's travel

Style Hunt

In the book *Call It Courage* by Armstrong Sperry, the reader is introduced to words from Mafatu's native language. Find the English meanings of the native words listed below. Write them in the spaces provided.

1. *tupapau* _____

2. *Ara Moana* _____

3. *fei* _____

4. *mo'o* _____

5. *pareau* _____

6. *puaa viri* _____

7. *purau* _____

8. *bonitos* _____

9. *himene* _____

10. *Maui* _____

Vocabulary Hunt

Find the following vocabulary words when reading *The Indian in the Cupboard* by Lynne Reid Banks.

Chapters 1–3 Clues   This one-syllable word is a homophone for a form of precipitation. It has a long **a** sound, but there is no a in the word.

Word _____ page _____

Chapters 4–6 Clues   This item can cure you. The word is in its plural form and contains two syllables.

Word _____ page _____

Chapters 7–9 Clues   This word means "gone into a trance." It contains the letter **z** in it and has three syllables.

Word _____ page _____

Chapters 10–12 Clues   Find a one-syllable word that means "imitate." It has the */aw/* sound.

Word _____ page _____

Chapters 13–14 Clues   This three-syllable word means "forever." The last three letters, when switched around, make a word.

Word _____ page _____

Chapters 15–16 Clues   This word means "right now." It has a double consonant and contains five syllables.

Word _____ page _____

Novel Hunt

Use a newspaper to find the following items from *The Indian in the Cupboard* by Lynne Reid Banks.

1. something that you put in a cupboard

2. any setting from the story

3. the word "little" or "bear"

4. first or last name of any character

5. something a cowboy needs

6. an item Little Bear used to build his house

7. what vittles are

8. a horse for sale

9. a picture of something a Native American uses

10. any food or beverage mentioned in the story

Style Hunt

Look up the word *stereotype* in your dictionary and write the definition in the space provided below.

stereotype _____

In Chapter Ten, there is a person who is stereotyped in *The Indian in the Cupboard* by Lynne Reid Banks. Find an example of a stereotype and write the sentence in the space provided below.

stereotype from Chapter Ten _____

_____

Think of someone or a class of people who have been stereotyped and write your example below.

_____

_____

Vocabulary Hunt

Find the following vocabulary words when reading *Julie of the Wolves* by Jean Craighead George.

Part One Clues

This compound word means "to play rigorously." It has two syllables.

Word _____ page _____

Part One Clues

This describes a tiny amount of food. This word has two vowels and two syllables.

Word _____ page _____

Part Two Clues

This word means "not paid attention to." It begins with a vowel and has two syllables.

Word _____ page _____

Part Two Clues

Find a word that names an information source. This word contains six syllables and five vowels.

Word _____ page _____

Part Three Clues

This is a hyphenated word that names a color, and it contains four syllables.

Word _____ page _____

Part Three Clues

Find a four-syllable plural word that describes a group of stars.

Word _____ page _____

Novel Hunt

Use a newspaper to find the following items from *Julie of the Wolves* by Jean Craighead George.

1. a city Julie wants to visit

2. the word "wilderness"

3. what a wolf eats

4. a word that describes Kapu, the wolf

5. any place in Alaska

6. something an Eskimo might use

7. the word "north"

8. something on the tundra

9. an animal from the story other than a wolf

10. a picture taken outdoors

Style Hunt

The author Jean Craighead George uses many descriptive passages in *Julie of the Wolves*. Reread the third paragraph in Part One. Find adverbs or adjectives the author uses to describe the following words for questions 1-5. In questions 6-10, find your own adverbs or adjectives to fill in the blanks that correspond to the nouns given.

1. _____ flowers

2. _____ briefly

3. _____ land

4. _____ flowers

5. _____ clouds

6. _____ weather

7. _____ storm

8. _____ horizon

9. _____ night

10. _____ walk

Vocabulary Hunt

Find the following vocabulary words when reading *My Brother Sam Is Dead* by James Lincoln Collier and Christopher Collier.

Chapters 1–2 Clues   This word means "to fool with." It has a double consonant and two syllables.

Word _____ page _____

Chapters 3–4 Clues   This two-syllable, compound word describes adults.

Word _____ page _____

Chapters 5–6 Clues   Find a three-syllable, compound word that describes those who are not expected to win.

Word _____ page _____

Chapters 7–8 Clues   This describes the number of people in a given area. It has two long vowel sounds and contains four syllables.

Word _____ page _____

Chapter 9–10 Clues   Find a word that means a surprise attack. It ends with the /sh/ sound and has two syllables.

Word _____ page _____

Chapters 11–13 Clues   This describes a quickly spreading disease. Every other letter is a consonant, and it has four syllables.

Word _____ page _____

Novel Hunt

Use a newspaper to find the following items from *My Brother Sam Is Dead* by James Lincoln Collier and Christopher Collier.

1. first name of any fictitious character in the story

2. what the Old Brown Bess is

3. book setting, a colony

4. color of lobsterback uniforms

5. who the colonists fought (a country or person)

6. book setting, a city

7. last name of a nonfictitious character

8. what Old Pru is

9. Sam's age

10. a form of colonial transportation

Style Hunt

Look up the word *metaphor* in your dictionary and write the definition in the space provided below.

metaphor _____

_____

Find a metaphor from Chapter 12 in *My Brother Sam is Dead* by James Lincoln Collier and Christopher Collier. Write the metaphor in the space provided below.

metaphor from Chapter 12_____

_____

Think of another example of a metaphor and write it below.

_____

_____

Vocabulary Hunt

Find the following vocabulary words when reading *Hatchet* by Gary Paulsen.

Chapters 1–3 Clues   This word means "huge," it has a double consonant, and it contains two syllables.

Word _____ page _____

Chapters 4–6 Clues   Find a three-syllable word that describes a flavor. The last four letters make a word.

Word _____ page _____

Chapters 7–9 Clues   This word means "able to start on fire." It has a double consonant and contains three syllables.

Word _____ page _____

Chapters 10–13 Clues   The first four letters of this word are a precious metal. The last three letters are an animal's home, and it contains two syllables.

Word _____ page _____

Chapters 14–16 Clues   This three-syllable word means "to think very deeply." It has the long **a** sound.

Word _____ page _____

Chapters 17–19 Clues   This word means "very tired." It has a prefix and a suffix and contains three syllables.

Word _____ page _____

Novel Hunt

Use a newspaper to find the following items mentioned in *Hatchet* by Gary Paulsen.

1. any part from an airplane (word or picture)

2. shape of the lake

3. setting of the story (country)

4. food that turtles supplied

5. a food that Brian craved from the city (word or picture)

6. any animal from the story

7. time when mosquitos come out

8. first name of book's author

9. something in the survival pack

10. what Brian's dad invented

Style Hunt

In *Hatchet*, Gary Paulsen uses a style of writing called *repetition*. Throughout the novel, key words are repeated over and over again. Think of three of these words that the author uses more than one time in the novel and list them below. After you list the word, state its importance to the story.

word_____why it is important_____

_____

word_____why it is important_____

_____

word_____why it is important_____

_____

Vocabulary Hunt

Find the following vocabulary words when reading *The Sign of the Beaver* by Elizabeth George Speare.

Chapters 1–4 Clues   This word means "urged." It has an **x** in it and begins with the /k/ sound.

Word _____ page _____

Chapters 5–9 Clues   This compound word with two syllables describes a place to learn.

Word _____ page _____

Chapters 10–13 Clues   This word means "throwing away." It has a prefix and a suffix, and it contains three syllables.

Word _____ page _____

Chapters 14–17 Clues   Find a word with a double-consonant that means "vanished." It contains a prefix and a suffix.

Word _____ page _____

Chapters 18–22 Clues   This two-syllable word means "very old." It begins with the long **a** sound.

Word _____ page _____

Chapters 23–25 Clues   This word describes an evening meal. It has a double consonant and two syllables.

Word _____ page _____

Novel Hunt

Use the newspaper to find the following items from *The Sign of the Beaver* by Elizabeth George Speare.

1. an animal that Attean hunted

2. Attean's fishing tool

3. setting of the story (a state name)

4. something that Matt's father left behind

5. name of the rifle thief

6. an Indian food

7. *aremus* in English

8. chased Matt from the trees

9. broke into the cabin

10. name of Matt's sister

Style Hunt

Look up the word *dialect* in your dictionary and write the definition in the space provided below.

dialect_____

_____

In *The Sign of the Beaver* by Elizabeth George Speare, find an example where a dialect is used by one of the book's characters and write it in the space provided below.

dialect from Chapter Three _____

_____

Think of a dialect that you use that may be different from what is considered standard English language and write it below.

your own dialect_____

_____

Vocabulary Hunt

Find the following vocabulary words when reading *A Wrinkle in Time* by Madeline L'Engle.

Chapters 1–2 Clues   Find a word that describes a feeling of displeasure toward another. It has a suffix and a prefix and contains three syllables.

Word _____ page _____

Chapters 3–4 Clues   This describes a pleasant odor. It has the long **a** sound, and it contains two syllables.

Word _____ page _____

Chapters 5–6 Clues   This describes a road surface. It has the long **a** sound and two syllables.

Word _____ page _____

Chapters 7–8 Clues   This word means "sad." It has the /aw/ sound and contains two syllables.

Word _____ page _____

Chapters 9–10 Clues   Find a two-syllable compound word that means "bad dreams."

Word _____ page _____

Chapters 11–12 Clues   This word means "slowly turned to liquid." It has a double consonant and contains two syllables.

Word _____ page _____

Novel Hunt

Use a newspaper to find the following items from *A Wrinkle in Time* by Madeline L'Engle.

1. what Mr. Murray studied

2. word describing the weather in Chapter One

3. the words "Mrs." and "who"

4. what Fortinbras is

5. the color of Mrs. Murray's hair

6. short name of person who held Mr. Murray captive

7. how Meg felt about herself in Chapter One

8. any setting from the story

9. what Uriel is

10. a sport Calvin liked

Style Hunt

Look up the word *proverb* in your dictionary and write the definition in the space provided below.

proverb_____

_____

Find a proverb in the book *A Wrinkle in Time* by Madeleine L'Engle and write it in the space provided below.

proverb from *A Wrinkle in Time*_____

_____

In the space below, give a literal translation of what the proverb means.

_____

_____

Vocabulary Hunt

Find the following vocabulary words when reading *Danny, the Champion of the World,* by Roald Dahl.

Chapters 1–3 Clues   This word means "sure to happen." It has a prefix and a suffix and contains five syllables.

Word _____ page _____

Chapters 4–5 Clues   This word means "once in a while." It has two sets of double consonants and contains five syllables.

Word _____ page _____

Chapters 6–8 Clues   Find a three-syllable word that means "exactly." It has a prefix and a suffix.

Word _____ page _____

Chapters 9–12 Clues   This word means "to hate." It has the long **i** sound and contains two syllables.

Word _____ page _____

Chapters 13–16 Clues   Find a word that has a double consonant and two syllables and means "very large."

Word _____ page _____

Chapters 17–22 Clues   This two-syllable word describes a color, and the last letter is a **t**.

Word _____ page _____

Novel Hunt

Use a newspaper to find the following items from *Danny, the Champion of the World* by Roald Dahl.

1. what Mr. Snoddy drank

2. best color to wear while poaching

3. first name of the Austin automobile

4. the word "champion"

5. what William worked on (word or picture)

6. Cox's orange pippins, the common name

7. any book setting

8. word that describes the keeper

9. what William broke

10. first name of any character

Style Hunt

Look up the word *onomatopoeia* in your dictionary and write the definition in the space provided below.

onomatopoeia _____

_____

Find two examples of onomatopoeia from Chapters 12 and 16 in the book *Danny, the Champion of the World* by Roald Dahl. Write them below.

onomatopoeia from Chapter 12 _____

onomatopoeia from Chapter 16 _____

Think of your own example of onomatopoeia and write it on the lines below.

_____

Vocabulary Hunt

Find the following vocabulary words when reading *Charlotte's Web* by E. B. White.

Chapters 1–3 Clues   This word means "to stare at." It has the same number of vowels and consonants and contains one syllable.

Word _____ page _____

Chapters 4–6 Clues   Find a word that describes a type of insect. The first four letters are a coin, and it has three syllables.

Word _____ page _____

Chapters 7–10 Clues   This compound word with two syllables describes a kind of weapon.

Word _____ page _____

Chapters 11–13 Clues   This describes a color. It has the long **e** sound and contains one syllable.

Word _____ page _____

Chapters 14–17 Clues   This three-syllable word means "able to do anything." The last four letters are something you put on a floor.

Word _____ page _____

Chapters 18–22 Clues   This word means "shook." It has a suffix and contains two syllables.

Word _____ page _____

Novel Hunt

Use a newspaper to find the following items from *Charlotte's Web* by E. B. White.

1. something you would find on a farm

2. proper name of one of the animals

3. something you see at the fair

4. where Charlotte made her web

5. common name of any animal from the story

6. last name of the author

7. what Templeton is

8. what a spider makes

9. season when baby spiders are born

10. a meat that could be made from Wilbur (word or picture)

Style Hunt

Look up the word *genre* in your dictionary and write the definition in the space provided below.

genre _____

_____

Study different types of genre. What genre do you think *Charlotte's Web* by E.B. White belongs to? _____

_____

State below the reasons for placing this story in the genre you chose.

_____

_____

Vocabulary Hunt

Find the following vocabulary words when reading *Island of the Blue Dolphins* by Scott O'Dell.

Chapters 1–5 Clues   This is an animal skin. It has one vowel and contains one syllable.

Word _____ page _____

Chapters 6–10 Clues   Find a two-syllable word that means "summoned." The last three letters spell a man's name.

Word _____ page _____

Chapters 11–15 Clues   This word means "chewed on." The first letter is silent, and it has one syllable.

Word _____ page _____

Chapters 16–20 Clues   This one-syllable word describes a flat spot on a cliff. It has the /j/ sound.

Word _____ page _____

Chapters 21–25 Clues   This is facial hair. It has the short **i** sound and contains two syllables.

Word _____ page _____

Chapters 26–29 Clues   This word means "to be grounded without escape." It has a suffix and two syllables.

Word _____ page _____

Novel Hunt

Use a newspaper to find the following items from *Island of the Blue Dolphins* by Scott O'Dell.

1. any kind of fish

2. a prominent geographic feature on the island

3. any place in Russia

4. the name of the ocean where the island is located

5. the word "ship"

6. an island from a map

7. something that is blue

8. what Rontu is

9. a word describing the island weather

10. the name of "the star that does not move"

Style Hunt

Look for examples of figurative language in *Island of the Blue Dolphins* by Scott O'Dell. Write each example in the spaces provided below.

a metaphor from Chapter Two _____

_____

an example of personification from Chapter Seven_____

_____

an example of onomatopoeia from Chapter 19 _____

_____

a simile from Chapter 21 _____

_____

Vocabulary Hunt

Find the following vocabulary words when reading *Sarah, Plain and Tall* by Patricia MacLachlan.

Chapters 1-2 Clues   This word means "very lively." The middle letter is a **g**, and it has four syllables.

Word _____ page _____

Chapter 3 Clues   This word describes a type of lady's hat. It has a double consonant and two syllables.

Word _____ page _____

Chapter 4 Clues   This is a smooth material. It has one vowel and one syllable.

Word _____ page _____

Chapter 5 Clues   This compound word with two syllables describes the tool used to stack hay.

Word _____ page _____

Chapters 6-7 Clues   This is a yellow summer plant. The last five letters spell a kind of animal, and it contains four syllables.

Word _____ page _____

Chapters 8–9 Clues   This word means "unwillingly." It has a double consonant and three syllables.

Word _____ page _____

Novel Hunt

Use a newspaper to find the following items from *Sarah, Plain and Tall* by Patricia MacLachlan.

1. one of the sea colors: blue, gray, or green

2. what Seal is

3. the color of Indian paintbrush

4. any animal mentioned in the story

5. a setting from the story

6. first name of any of the characters

7. one of Sarah's skills

8. the state Sarah came from

9. a gift that Sarah brought

10. color of Sarah's bonnet

Style Hunt

Look up the word *personification* in your dictionary and write the definition in the space provided below.

personification _____

_____

Find an example of personification in Chapter One of *Sarah, Plain and Tall* by Patricia MacLachlan. Write the sentence in the space provided below.

personification from Chapter One. _____

_____

Make up your own example of personification and write it below.

your own example of personification _____

_____

Vocabulary Hunt

Find the following vocabulary words when reading *Bridge to Terabithia* by Katherine Patterson.

Chapters 1–2 Clues   This word means "to throw away." It has a prefix and contains two syllables.

Word _____ page _____

Chapters 3–4 Clues   This adverb with three syllables means "to do something without wanting to."

Word _____ page _____

Chapters 5–6 Clues   This two-syllable word means "three." It has the same number of vowels and consonants.

Word _____ page _____

Chapters 7–8 Clues   Find a word that describes a small amount of moving water. It has the short **i** sound and contains two syllables.

Word _____ page _____

Chapters 9–10 Clues   This is a color. This word has more vowels than consonants and contains one syllable.

Word _____ page _____

Chapters 11–13 Clues   This three-syllable word means "tightening." It has a prefix and a suffix.

Word _____ page _____

Novel Hunt

Use a newspaper to find the following items from *Bridge to Terabithia* by Katherine Patterson.

1. one-word theme of this story

2. a game mentioned in the story

3. what Miss Bessie is

4. a bridge (word or picture)

5. Janice Avery's physical stature

6. Miss Edmunds' job

7. first name of any character from the story

8. Jesse's hobby

9. any story setting

10. what Prince Terrien is

Style Hunt

Look for examples of figurative language in *Bridge to Terabithia* by Katherine Patterson. Write each example in the spaces provided below.

a simile from Chapter Four _____

_____

an example of personification from Chapter Four _____

_____

a metaphor from Chapter Five_____

_____

an example of onomatopoeia from Chapter Eight_____

_____

an idiom from Chapter Eight _____

_____

Vocabulary Hunt

Find the following vocabulary words when reading *Henry Huggins* by Beverly Cleary.

Chapter 1 Clues   This word means "persons who take a ride in a vehicle." It has a double consonant and three syllables.

Word _____ page _____

Chapter 2 Clues   This is a measure of temperature. It uses the same vowel three times and contains two syllables.

Word _____ page _____

Chapter 3 Clues   Find a one-syllable word that means "went by quickly." It has a double consonant.

Word _____ page _____

Chapter 4 Clues   This word means "very soft," ends with the long **e** sound, and has three syllables.

Word _____ page _____

Chapter 5 Clues   This compound word with two syllables means "to put off until later."

Word _____ page _____

Chapter 6 Clues   This is a border on a street. It has the */er/* sound and contains one syllable.

Word _____ page _____

Novel Hunt

Use a newspaper to find the following items from *Henry Huggins* by Beverly Cleary.

1. the color of the guppies

2. the word "bus"

3. any setting from the story

4. something Ribsy would eat (word or picture)

5. who Henry got a ride from

6. any type of dog

7. how much Henry paid for the guppies

8. first or last name of any character

9. a word that describes Scooter

10. an animal Henry does not own

Style Hunt

Look up the word *derogatory* in your dictionary and write the definition in the space provided below.

derogatory _____

_____

Find where derogatory language is used in Chapter Six of *Henry Huggins* by Beverly Cleary. Write that passage in the space provided below.

derogatory passage from Chapter Six_____

_____

How might a derogatory statement such as the one found in Chapter Six make one feel? Write your feelings on the lines below.

your own example _____

_____

Vocabulary Hunt

Find the following vocabulary words when reading *The Lion, the Witch and the Wardrobe* by
C. S. Lewis.

Chapters 1–3 Clues   This is a another word for a joke. It has the long **o** sound
and contains one syllable.

Word _____ page _____

Chapters 4–6 Clues   This is a three-syllable word for a pair of glasses. It has
the short **e** sound.

Word _____ page _____

Chapters 7–9 Clues   Find a one-syllable word that describes where a king sits.
It has the long **o** sound.

Word _____ page _____

Chapters 10–12 Clues   This one-syllable word describes a weak wind. It uses the
same vowel three times.

Word _____ page _____

Chapters 13–15 Clues   This word means "to give up." The first three letters are a
word, and it has two syllables.

Word _____ page _____

Chapters 16–17 Clues   This is another word for prey. It has a double consonant,
and it contains two syllables.

Word _____ page _____

Novel Hunt

Use a newspaper to find the following items from *The Lion, the Witch and the Wardrobe* by C. S. Lewis.

1. first name of any story character

2. a word that describes the professor

3. something that you could put in a wardrobe

4. a setting in the story

5. number of people who notice the kids are missing

6. form of precipitation mentioned in the story

7. a word that describes Aslan

8. any animal mentioned in the book

9. a homophone for witch

10. a picture of another Lucy from the comics

Style Hunt

Look up the word *sarcasm* in your dictionary and write the definition in the space provided below.

sarcasm _____

_____

Find an example of sarcasm in the book *The Lion, the Witch and the Wardrobe* by C. S. Lewis. Write this example of sarcasm in the space provided below.

example of sarcasm from Chapter 11 _____

_____

Think of your own example of sarcasm and write it below.

your own example _____

_____

Vocabulary Hunt

Find the following vocabulary words when reading *Little House on the Prairie* by Laura Ingalls Wilder.

Chapters 1–4 Clues   This two-syllable word is another word for horses. It has the long **a** sound.

Word _____ page _____

Chapters 5–8 Clues   This word means "talked softly." The last three letters are a color, and it has two syllables.

Word _____ page _____

Chapters 9–12 Clues   This two-syllable word means "to be without clothes." It has the long **a** sound.

Word _____ page _____

Chapters 13–17 Clues   Find a word that means "walked on hands and knees." The last three letters are a word.

Word _____ page _____

Chapters 18–22 Clues   This is another word for a thick soup or a soft food. It has a double consonant and two syllables.

Word _____ page _____

Chapters 23–26 Clues   This is another word for an idea. It has the long **o** sound, and it has two syllables.

Word _____ page _____

Novel Hunt

Use a newspaper to find the following items from *Little House on the Prairie* by Laura Ingalls Wilder.

1. something you could find on the prairie

2. what Jack is

3. a crop the family planted (word or picture)

4. first name of any story character

5. where the family got their drinking water

6. a state that has a prairie

7. any food mentioned in the story

8. what Bunny is

9. any wild animal (word or picture)

10. a word that describes Pa

Style Hunt

Look up the word *hyperbole* in your dictionary and write the definition in the space provided below.

hyperbole _____

_____

In Chapter 15 in the book *Little House on the Prairie* by Laura Ingalls Wilder, find an example of hyperbole. Write this example in the space provided below.

example of hyperbole from Chapter 15 _____

_____

Think of your own example of hyperbole and write it below.

your own example _____

_____

Vocabulary Hunt

Find the following vocabulary words when reading *The Whipping Boy* by Sid Fleischman.

Chapters 1–3 Clues   This two-syllable word means "trouble." It has a prefix.

Word _____ page _____

Chapters 4–6 Clues   This is a ruthless person. It is a compound word with two syllables.

Word _____ page _____

Chapters 7–8 Clues   This two-syllable word describes a child without a home. The first two letters are a word.

Word _____ page _____

Chapters 9–12 Clues   This is money or valuables to be traded for someone kidnapped. The first three letters are a word, and there are two syllables.

Word _____ page _____

Chapters 13–16 Clues   This one-syllable word means "to desperately be in need of food." It has the /ar/ sound.

Word _____ page _____

Chapters 17–19 Clues   Find a three-syllable word that means lack of knowledge. It has the /or/ sound.

Word _____ page _____

Novel Hunt

Use a newspaper to find the following items from *The Whipping Boy* by Sid Fleischman.

1. a word that describes Jemmy

2. any kind of food mentioned in the story

3. the first name of any character

4. what Petunia is

5. a place where Jemmy hides

6. any outdoor setting from the story

7. a ransom material from the book

8. any royal word

9. a word that means whip

10. a word that describes the prince

Style Hunt

Look up the word *simile* in your dictionary and write the definition in the space provided below.

simile _____

_____

Find a simile in the book *The Whipping Boy* by Sid Fleischman. Write the sentence in the space provided below.

a simile in Chapter One _____

_____

Make up a simile of your own and write it below.

your own simile _____

_____

Vocabulary Hunt

Find the following vocabulary words when reading *The Midwife's Apprentice* by Karen Cushman.

Chapters 1–3 Clues   This is the top of a room. It has the long **e** sound and contains two syllables.

Word _____ page _____

Chapters 4–6 Clues   This four-syllable word means "to go somewhere with someone." It has a double consonant.

Word _____ page _____

Chapters 7–9 Clues   This three-syllable word means "very fragile."

Word _____ page _____

Chapters 10–12 Clues   This word means "cleaning thoroughly." It has a suffix and contains two syllables.

Word _____ page _____

Chapters 13–15 Clues   This is another name for "bricklayers." It has the long **a** sound and contains two syllables.

Word _____ page _____

Chapters 16–17 Clues   This three-syllable word means "not guilty." It has a double consonant.

Word _____ page _____

Novel Hunt

Use a newspaper to find the following items from *The Midwife's Apprentice* by Karen Cushman.

1. an animal mentioned in the story

2. color of Will's hair

3. the most beautiful letter

4. what a midwife helps with (word or picture)

5. what Alyce Little is

6. the first name of any character in the story

7. any food mentioned in the story

8. color of sheep soap

9. any of the story's settings

10. Alyce' s opinion of herself in Chapter One

Style Hunt

Look up the word *alliteration* in your dictionary and write the definition in the space provided below.

alliteration _____

_____

Find an example of alliteration in *The Midwife's Apprentice* by Karen Cushman. Write the sentence in the space provided below.

alliteration in Chapter Nine _____

_____

Make up your own example of alliteration and write it below.

your own example of alliteration _____

_____

Vocabulary Hunt

Find the following vocabulary words when reading *The Call of the Wild* by Jack London.

Chapter 1 Clues   This word means "changed into something else." It has five vowels and four syllables.

Word _____ page _____

Chapter 2 Clues   This three-syllable word means "cleverly." It has a double consonant.

Word _____ page _____

Chapter 3 Clues   This is the very top of something. It has a double consonant and two syllables.

Word _____ page _____

Chapter 4 Clues   This one-syllable word describes the first part of the day. It has the /aw/ sound.

Word _____ page _____

Chapter 5 Clues   This compound word with three syllables means "very sad."

Word _____ page _____

Chapters 6-7 Clues   This three-syllable word means "to consider." The last five letters are something you can eat from.

Word _____ page _____

Novel Hunt

Use a newspaper to find the following items from *The Call of the Wild* by Jack London.

1. any weapon mentioned in the story

2. a word that describes the Yukon weather

3. something the dogs ate

4. the word "sled"

5. important human food

6. first name of any character

7. any story setting

8. a word that describes the rivers in the spring

9. what Buck is

10. direction of the Yukon from here

Style Hunt

Find an example of an idiom, a simile, a metaphor, and a hyperbole from *The Call of the Wild* by Jack London. Find examples of figurative language and write them in the spaces provided below.

an idiom from Chapter Seven _____

_____

a simile from Chapter Seven _____

_____

a metaphor from Chapter Seven _____

_____

hyperbole from Chapter Seven _____

_____

Newspaper Letter Count

Find a paragraph of reasonable length in the newspaper. Below is the listing of all the letters in the alphabet. Make tally marks by the letters below for each letter in the paragraph. Find the most frequently used letters in your paragraph. How many total letters are in the paragraph? What percent of the letters are "s"? Compare your findings with another member of your class.

a_____   n_____

b_____   o_____

c_____   p_____

d_____   q_____

e_____   r_____

f_____   s_____

g_____   t_____

h_____   u_____

i_____   v_____

j_____   w_____

k_____   x_____

l_____   y_____

m_____   z_____

The Mad Dash Word Hunt

Find in the newspaper as many of the words listed below as fast as you can. You will only have five minutes. Cut and glue the words on a piece of white paper.

eye	horse	recreation
blue	terror	the
lawyer	Atlanta	four
egg	green	shoes
building	occupation	sale
and	always	said
over	truck	also
between	state	remember
sincerely	comics	football
with	street	rear
afraid	taxi	an
coffee	tax	governor
animal	red	for
elderly	smoke	vacation
picture	belief	north
nine	life	year
only	television	relish
today	march	troops
man	conclusion	there
to	killed	senate
wisdom	occur	thief
rain	car	rich
sugar	gold	not
yesterday	iron	value

Alphabet Word Hunt

Find words that begin with each letter in the alphabet and glue them in the spaces provided below.

a _____   n _____

b _____   o _____

c _____   p _____

d _____   q _____

e _____   r _____

f _____   s _____

g _____   t _____

h _____   u _____

i _____   v _____

j _____   w _____

k _____   x _____

l _____   y _____

m _____   z _____

Newspaper Word Search

Use the grid below to play Newspaper Word Search. Choose nine words to build the puzzle, and write your words in the word box below. Cut out various sizes of newspaper letters and glue the words on the grid. Then surround other letters from the newspaper and glue those down as well. Give your word search to another student to try to solve.

Word Box

_____   _____   _____

_____   _____   _____

_____   _____   _____

Word Trees

Cut letters from a newspaper to complete the following word trees below. Look at the top letter on each of the word trees. Think of a two-letter word to go on the next line. For each word, you must use letters that are in the word at the bottom of the tree. After you use a letter, you must keep it in use for the next word on the tree. Then use another letter from the bottom of the tree to build the next word. You may want to work in reverse order, from the bottom up.

Example:

```
          o
        o   n
      n   o   n
    n   o   o   n
  o   n   i   o   n
```

1.
```
              a

        ____ ____

    ____ ____ ____ ____
     h    a    n    d
```

2.
```
          m

      ____ ____

    ____ ____ ____
     t    i    m    e
```

3.
```
              h

        ____ ____ ____

    ____ ____ ____ ____
     t    h    r    e    e
```

4.
```
          d

      ____ ____

    ____ ____ ____

  ____ ____ ____ ____
   w    o    u    l    d
```

5.
```
              o

        ____ ____

    ____ ____ ____
     f    o    r    t
```

Make Your Own Scavenger Hunt

Beside each number write your own Newspaper Scavenger Hunt clues. Try to think of items that you have learned in school. When you are finished, give it to one of your classmates. See how many of the items he or she can find.

1. _____
_____

2. _____
_____

3. _____
_____

4. _____
_____

5. _____
_____

6. _____
_____

7. _____
_____

8. _____
_____

9. _____
_____

10. _____
_____

Newspaper Word Hunt

1. Give each student a copy of the work sheet on page 124.

2. Have students cut letters from the newspaper and randomly glue them in boxes on the grid, one letter per box. Use boldface letters like those found in the headlines. Make sure students do not form words when they glue the letters on the grid. Have students include at least three vowels with the letters they choose and make sure that they do not use any letter more than once. Allow students to put letter sounds in the same box. For example, they may cut the /sh/ sound from a word in the headlines and put it in one of the boxes.

3. Collect the grids after students have completed step 2. Arrange students in groups of either two, three, or four players. Distribute one grid per group, facedown so that players cannot see the letters on the grid. Each player should have a pencil and piece of scratch paper.

4. On the word "GO" students will turn the grid over and find as many words as they can from the letters on the grid. Give students a specified amount of time to complete this task (start with a one-minute game and adjust if necessary).

5. After the time for writing words is over, have players read their list to the other players. If more than one player has a word, all players must scratch that word from their lists.

6. After all players in the group have read their lists, score the remaining words numerically as follows. For each letter in a remaining word, players will receive a point. For example, remaining one-letter words are worth one point. Remaining two-letter words are worth two points, etc. The player with the most points remaining is the winner.

Scoring Example:

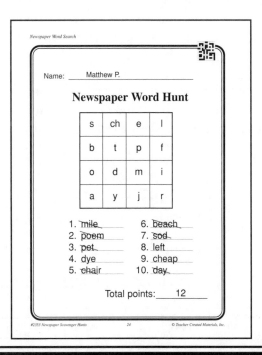

Newspaper Category Hunt

Think of different categories that might interest students and have them find as many matching items in the newspaper as they can. You may want to use areas of study as one of your categories. For example, if you are studying Mexico, ask students to find items in the paper that are relevant to this category. This might include words that have Spanish origins, Mexican foods, or any places in Mexico that are named in a newspaper.

Also use the Newspaper Category Hunt to enhance a language lesson. If you are studying adjectives, for example, you might ask students to find words used as nouns in the newspaper and adjectives that describe them. For math, have students make a list of prime numbers that they find in the newspaper. Use the work sheet on page 125 to help organize your Newspaper Category Hunt.

Newspaper Sentence Scramble

Make copies of the work sheet on page 126 using cardstock. Cut along the lines to make cards for Newspaper Sentence Scramble. Pass out ten cards per student. Have students find examples of the parts of speech in the newspaper; encourage the use of boldface type for this activity—such as the type found in headlines. Students will cut out these examples and glue them to their cards. Allow students to glue only one word per card unless they are finding verb phrases. In this case the entire verb phrase may be glued to the card. On the remaining cards, have students cut and glue commas, exclamation marks, periods, and question marks. On the backs of the cards, they will write which part of speech they have found.

Collect the cards by the parts of speech. Pick up the nouns first, then the verbs, etc. Keep the cards in separate piles. Then shuffle each pile and redistribute the cards to the class. Have the class practice arranging the cards into sentences. Allow trades to occur if students are having trouble making sentences.

Walk around the room and have students read completed sentences to the class. Collect the cards upon the completion of the activity and save them for future use. For younger students, glue letters on the cards and have the class form words for the letters after they are redistributed.

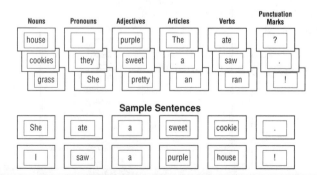

Crossword Pictures

Divide your class into groups or let individuals make their own crossword picture games. First, give each student or each group a copy of the work sheet on pages 127 and 128. Students will look through the newspaper and find interesting pictures that fit into the clue boxes, on the work sheet page 127. The pictures may be real, from cartoons, or other drawings found in the newspaper.

After students have found ten pictures to complete the clue sheet (work sheet, page 127) they will find spaces on the grid for each word that a picture describes. Each picture will have more than one possibility. For example, if a student put a picture of a truck on his or her picture clue sheet, he or she might want to allow space for the letters for "automobile" on the Crossword Picture Grid on page 128.

Encourage students to cross their letters through the letters of other words and build off other letters from other words much like an original crossword puzzle. When they have finished placing and numbering their grids with the appropriate letter spaces and numbers, students will darken the remaining spaces. Remember, page 128 will look much the same as an original crossword puzzle. Allow students to pass their clue sheets and crossword grids to other groups to solve.

Newspaper Word Find

Newspaper Word Find is played in groups of two. Each player starts with two blank copies of Newspaper Word Find Player Work Sheet page 129. Participants will use the newspaper to spell words to place on the grids. You may suggest that they cut individual letters from their newspapers to spell vocabulary words from a particular unit of study or use their weekly spelling words. Allow students to arrange from four to six words on the grid. Make sure that players understand that there may be only one letter per square on the grid.

When students are finished arranging their words on the grid, the first player will call out a coordinate. For example, player A might call "C4". Player B must tell player A whether she hit a square with a letter in it or hit a blank square. If player A hit a letter, player B must reveal the letter to her. On a blank grid, player A will tally the results by writing the letters she finds on the appropriate squares and placing an "X" in squares that she misses. Upon completion of one game, have students reverse roles, making player B call a coordinate while A keeps tally on the blank grid.

You may want to use this activity as a spare-time activity, assigning it early in the week as it is time consuming.

Newspaper Name Descriptions

Have each member of your class write his or her name vertically on an 8 ½" x 11" (22 cm x 28 cm) sheet of white paper using a black marker. Have students find words in the newspaper that describe themselves using words that begin with each letter of their names. Students will cut off the first letter of the words they find and glue the rest of the words by each letter in their names. For example, Tommy might find the word "tricky" in the headlines. He would cut off the "T" and glue the "ricky" part of the "T" in his name, Tommy. When students have finished, display the name descriptions throughout the room.

Newspaper Twenty Questions

Divide your classroom into two groups. Each group will find something hidden in the newspaper. You may want to limit the hidden objects to pictures or words in the headlines; otherwise, they may be too difficult to find. After each group has found their hidden object, one group gets to ask the other twenty "yes" or "no" questions that will help them locate the object. The asking group may begin by saying, "Is your object in the sports section?" The hiding group would have to answer "yes" or "no." Allow students time to plan a strategy before they begin asking questions. You should also make sure that each group has the same issue of a newspaper before beginning this activity.

Newspaper Relay

Hand out newspapers or sections of newspapers to each student in your class. Then give one student in the room a copy of the Newspaper Relay Work Sheet page 130. The first student will find a word in the newspaper, cut it out, and glue it on line number 1. He will then pass it to a student behind him. This student will find another word and glue it on line number 2. The class will try to make sentences as the Newspaper Relay Work Sheet goes from student to student. The activity ends when each student has had a turn to cut and paste a word. Smaller classes may need to pass the sheet around the room twice.

Read the story to your class upon completion.

Scavenger Art Hunt

Find the outlines beginning on page 132 of this book. Choose one that you feel is appropriate and make enough copies for each member of your class. Ask students to find in a newspaper as many words or pictures that are pertinent to the outline as they can find. Have students cut and glue the pictures and words that they find on the inside of the outline in any order they desire. For example, if you are using the football, students might look on the sports page and find team names, a cartoon drawing of a football, box scores, a picture of a football player, or other related items.

Also use the outlines to make newspaper collages. Use old newspapers cut into small pieces to fill in the outlines. Use a variety of colors and different types to give the outlines a unique appearance.

Bargain Hunts

Save as many food advertisements from large grocery stores as you need for your class. Break up your class into groups and tell students that they will have 25 dollars to feed a family of five people for an entire day. They must prepare at least three meals for the day. Each meal must have at least four food items including beverages. Students will cut out their chosen foods and glue each meal on a piece of paper—breakfast, lunch, and dinner. They may not exceed 25 dollars or the amount specified by the teacher.

Breakfast
eggs, toast, bacon, and juice

Lunch
tuna melt, soup, salad, and ice tea

Dinner
sirloin steak, green beans, rice, and soda

Daily Total _____

BUY ONE, GET ONE FREE!

SIRLOIN STEAK

Upon completion of the activity, review the results and discuss what the families had to eat for the amount of money they had to spend. How much would it cost the same family to eat for one month? for one year? Did the family eat modestly, or was there enough money to spend on luxury items?

Have all students use the newspaper to plan a family vacation for the same family. Find the prices of airline tickets, lodging, food, and activities. How far could the family go on a budget of 1,000 dollars? How many days could the family spend away from home? Give your class hypothetical amounts of money and different scenarios to generate interesting discussions.

Name: _____

Newspaper Word Hunt
Work Sheet

1. _____   6. _____
2. _____   7. _____
3. _____   8. _____
4. _____   9. _____
5. _____   10. _____

Total points: _____

Newspaper Category Hunt
Work Sheet

Category Hunt name of category_____	**Category Hunt** name of category_____

Newspaper Sentence Scramble

Crossword Picture Work Sheet

Clues Going Across	Clues Going Down
1.	1.
2.	2.
3.	3.
4.	4.
5.	5.

Crossword Picture Grid

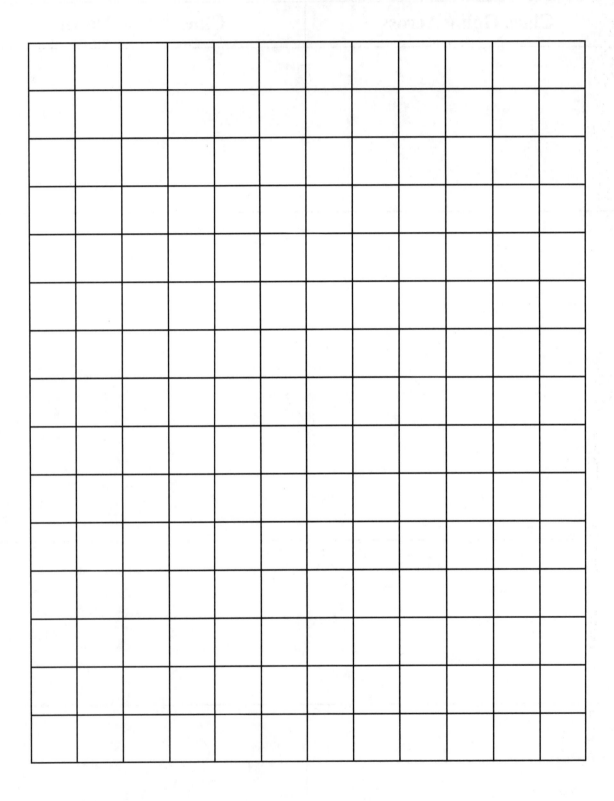

Newspaper Word Find Work Sheet

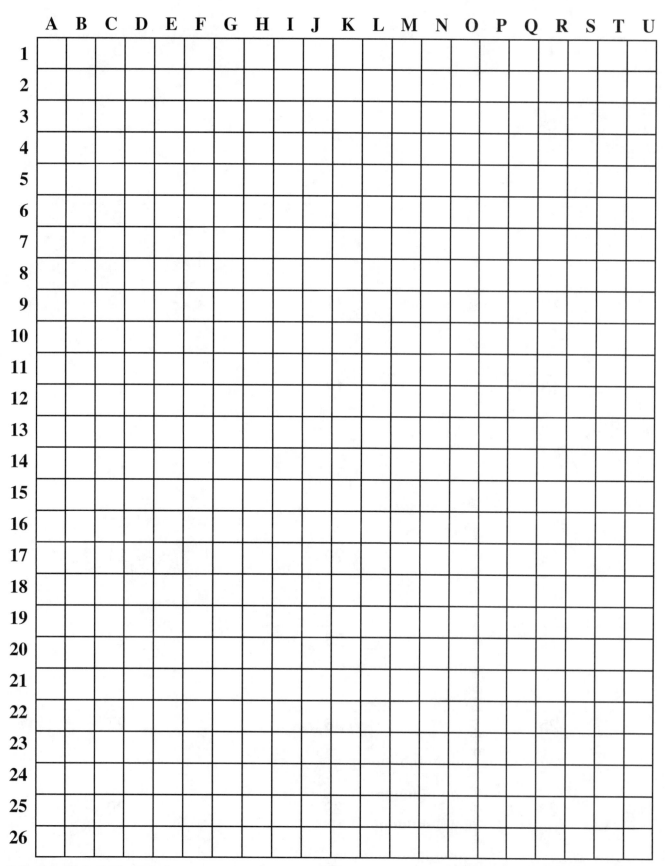

Newspaper Relay Work Sheet

1	2	3
4	5	6
7	8	9
10	11	12
13	14	15
16	17	18
19	20	21
22	23	24
25	26	27
28	29	30

Newspaper Scavenger Hunt
Work Sheet

1.	6.
2.	7.
3.	8.
4.	9.
5.	10.

Note: this work sheet is for Scavenger, Content, and Novel Hunt activities

Scavenger Art Hunt
Bat and Ball

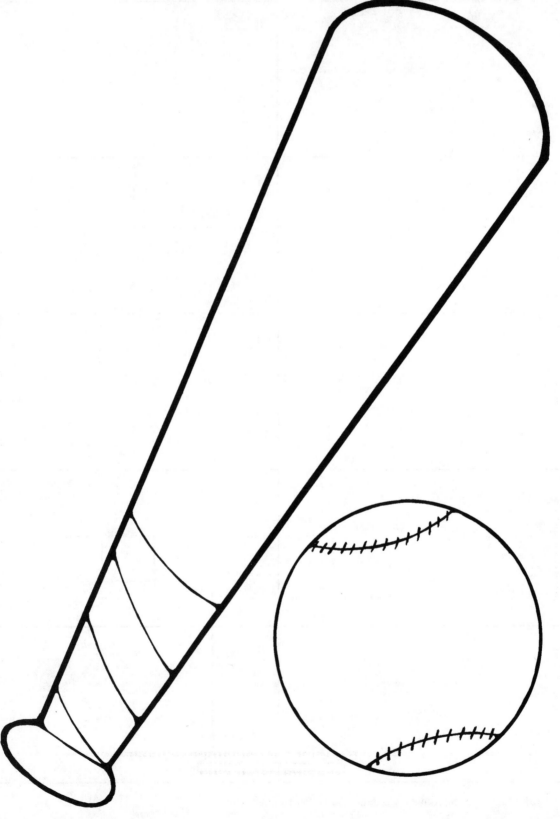

Scavenger Art Hunt
House

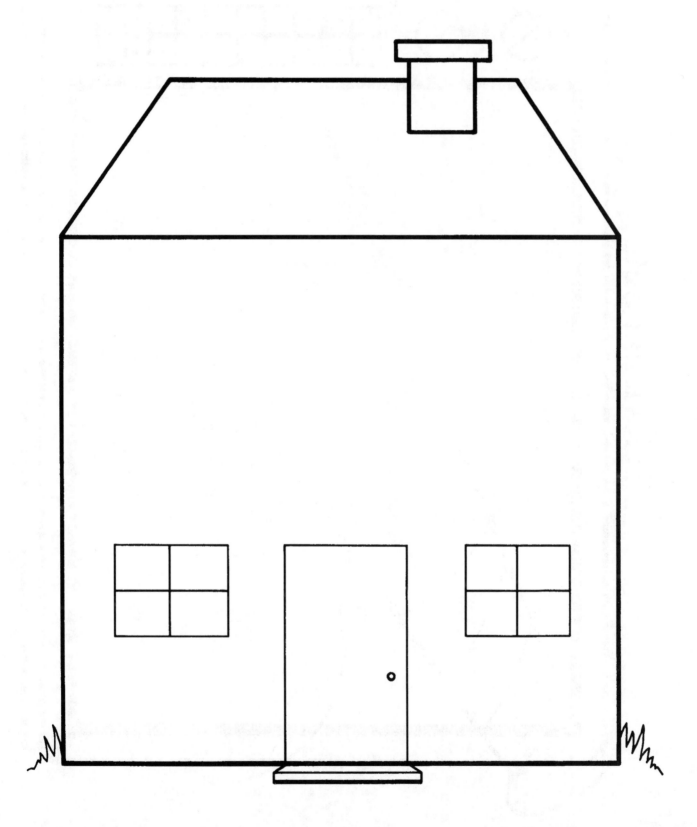

Scavenger Art Hunt

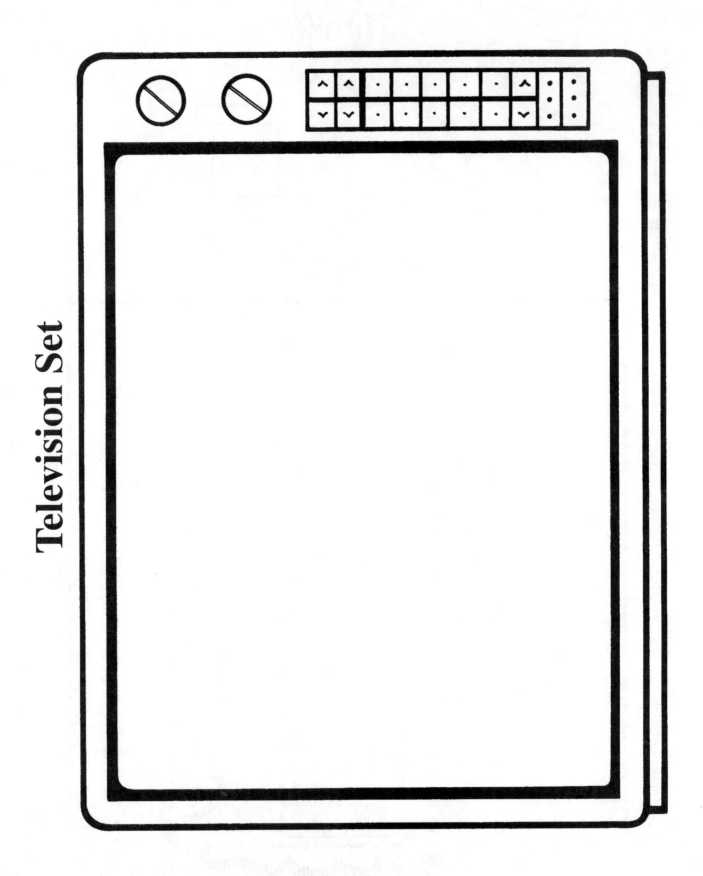

Television Set

Scavenger Art Hunt
Owl

Scavenger Art Hunt
Musical Note

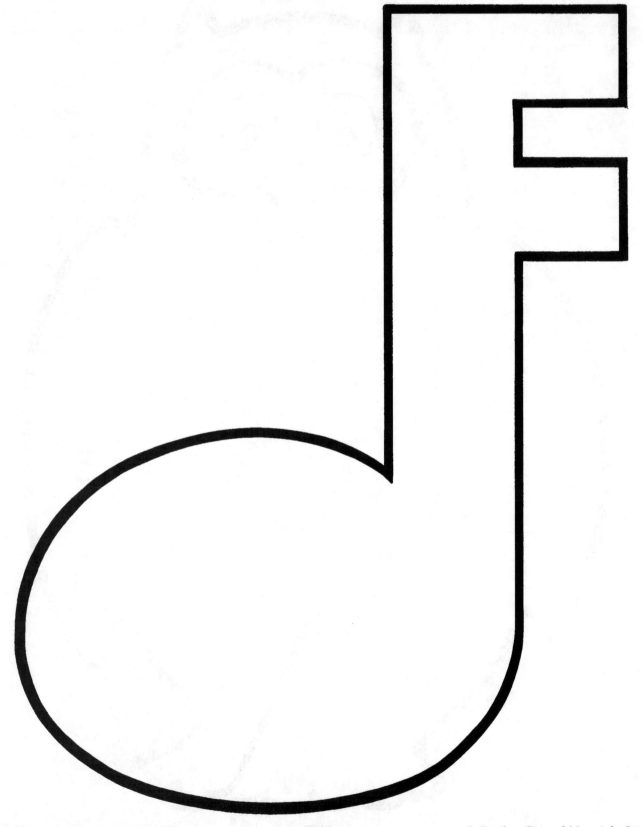

Scavenger Art Hunt

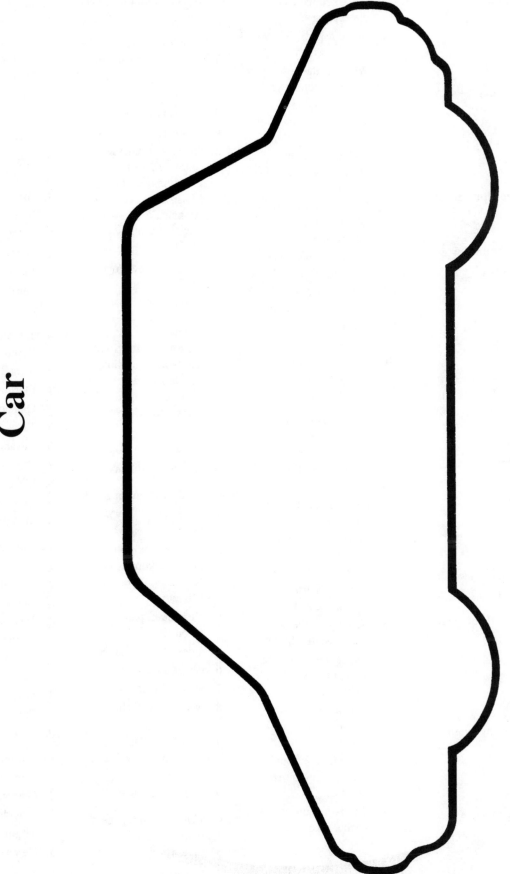

Car

Answer Key

Homophone Hunt, page 31

1. course
2. peer
3. through
4. read
5. here
6. two or too
7. feat
8. toad
9. their or they're
10. way

Homophone Hunt, page 31

1. flower
2. four
3. there or they're
4. principal
5. flew
6. to or too
7. read
8. sweet
9. meat
10. beat

Abbreviation Hunt, page 34

1. hour
2. quart
3. apartment
4. avenue
5. ounce
6. year
7. pound
8. dozen
9. company
10. weight

Conjunction Hunt, page 41

1. and
2. or
3. but (or *and*)
4. and
5. but (or *and*)
6. and (or the word *or*)
7. and
8. but
9. or
10. and

Punctuation Hunt, page 42

1. We asked the clerk for the catalog.
2. Marie asked, "Did you find the watch yet?"
3. Where is the bus going to stop first?
4. Oh my goodness! The picture turned out horribly.
5. "Where is the best place to eat?" asked Margie.
6. I do not understand why he wants us to follow him.
7. What a tremendous effort he displayed!
8. I think Benedict Arnold was a traitor.
9. My address is P.O. Box 456.
10. The St. Louis Blues are my favorite hockey team.

Capital Letter Hunt, page 42

1. Many professional players live in Washington, D.C.
2. The Mississippi River is among the largest in America.
3. I have always admired Mr. Johnson for his courage.
4. The best houses are on Jones Creek.
5. He lives on the north side of Sutton Street.
6. Sergeant MacDonald lives in the Smith Barracks.
7. The capital of Wyoming is Cheyenne.
8. I. B. M. makes excellent computer systems.
9. Our barn is on Ryeburg Road.

10. The tree by the fence is a memorial to Miss Coughlin.

Social Studies Hunt, page 43

1. George or Washington
2. Oklahoma, Kansas, Texas
3. Answers will vary.
4. Answers will vary.
5. Georgia, Tennessee, South or North Carolina, Florida, Mississippi, Virginia, Alabama, Louisiana, Texas, Arkansas
6. tax
7. Virginia, New York, Vermont, New Hampshire, Pennsylvania, Delaware, Massachusetts, South and North Carolina, Rhode Island, Connecticut, Maryland, Maine
8. 18
9. Answers will vary.
10. Answers will vary.

Social Studies Hunt, page 43

1. Answers will vary.
2. logs, tools, etc.
3. Montana, North or South Dakota, Kansas, Nebraska, Wyoming, Missouri
4. aluminum, paper, wood, etc.
5. a desert, Arizona, etc.
6. cars, factories, etc.
7. answers will vary
8. bus, airplane, ship, etc.
9. Presidents' Day, Columbus Day, Labor Day, etc.
10. flag, eagle, etc.

City Nickname Hunt, page 45

1. Paris
2. Philadelphia
3. Chicago

4. San Antonio
5. San Francisco
6. Denver
7. Los Angeles
8. Seattle
9. Dallas
10. New York

Country Hunt, page 45

1. Russia
2. Kenya
3. Spain
4. Brazil
5. France
6. Norway
7. Germany
8. India
9. Australia
10. Japan

State Nickname Hunt, page 46

1. Kentucky
2. Iowa
3. Florida
4. Oklahoma
5. Texas
6. Nevada
7. Pennsylvania
8. Idaho
9. New Jersey
10. Michigan

State Nickname Hunt, page 46

1. Utah
2. Hawaii
3. Delaware
4. Tennessee
5. Illinois
6. New York
7. North Carolina
8. Montana
9. California
10. Wisconsin

State/Capital Hunt, page 47

1. North Dakota
2. Oregon
3. Providence
4. Virginia
5. New York

Answer Key *(cont.)*

6. Delaware
7. Lincoln
8. Minnesota
9. Cheyenne
10. Kentucky

State Capital Hunt, page 47
1. Boise
2. Indianapolis
3. Vermont
4. Columbus
5. Denver
6. Louisiana
7. Maine
8. Jackson
9. North Carolina
10. Washington

Science Hunt, page 48
1. oxygen, hydrogen, etc.
2. rubber, glass, etc.
3. cake mix
4. Answers will vary.
5. iron, steel, metal, etc.
6. humidity
7. copper, etc.
8. oil, soap, etc.
9. 79
10. hair, carpet, etc.

Biology Hunt, page 48
1. snake, lizard, etc.
2. ocean
3. any fruit or grain
4. nitrogen, etc.
5. soil, grass, etc.
6. calcium, iron, etc.
7. ph
8. *x* or *y*
9. human, deer, etc.
10. a fish

Math Hunt, page 49
1. 12
2. 9
3. 2, 2, 5
4. 60
5. ex: 567
6. Answers will vary.
7. ex: 31
8. Answers will vary.

9. 45
10. 200

Animal Hunt, page 51
1. cow
2. any hoofed animal
3. Answers will vary.
4. any animal that eats all foods
5. any animal that lives on land and water
6. Answers will vary.
7. any animal that eats only plants
8. any bird of prey
9. deer, elk, etc.
10. meat eater

Newspaper Hunt, page 53
1. writing under a picture
2. boldface print above an article
3. the name of an author
4. box containing information about the newspaper
5. a notice of a person's death
6. a story with the letters **AP** before it
7. capital letters at the beginning of the article that tell where the article came from
8. newspaper's front-page logo
9. a story's first paragraph
10. a story that is continued

Letter Hunt #1, page 66
1. hat
2. kitten
3. grass
4. glass
5. sun
6. ship
7. out
8. penny
9. fly
10. giggle

Letter Hunt #2, page 66
1. ape
2. skinny
3. wind
4. crown
5. axe
6. head
7. supper
8. orange
9. late
10. baa

Answer Key *(cont.)*

Letter Hunt #3, page 67

1. mold
2. pillow
3. home
4. yes
5. tom
6. smile
7. fawn
8. hand
9. club
10. circus

Letter Hunt #4, page 67

1. three
2. are
3. igloo
4. scissors
5. calf
6. bow
7. net
8. odd
9. pine
10. Pole

Letter Hunt #5, page 68

1. narrow
2. swan
3. oar
4. few
5. canoe
6. tennis
7. alley
8. rarely
9. zero
10. log

Letter Hunt #6, page 68

1. sleep
2. cafe
3. pencil
4. tight
5. near
6. toss
7. ruler
8. shore
9. model
10. solo

Letter Hunt #7, page 69

1. ash
2. ace
3. guitar
4. plain
5. helium
6. pickle
7. June
8. opera
9. rye
10. diet

Letter Hunt #8, page 69

1. avalanche
2. towel
3. harmonica
4. radio
5. tart
6. boxes
7. lamp
8. harem
9. gloves
10. sheriff

Letter Hunt #9, page 70

1. settlement
2. roast
3. inn
4. pins
5. flashlight
6. clown
7. collect
8. bother
9. sharp
10. polo

Letter Hunt #10, page 70

1. apologize
2. sugar
3. village
4. rooster
5. glorious
6. grizzly
7. quarter
8. dinner
9. mustache
10. warranty

Letter Hunt #11, page 71

1. classified
2. colt
3. site
4. versatile
5. durable
6. volume
7. misplace
8. relocate
9. smooth
10. fluids

Letter Hunt #12, page 71

1. complain
2. meteor
3. license
4. plague
5. mezzo
6. hasty
7. obituary
8. mention
9. midnight
10. hardware

Letter Hunt #13, page 72

1. chimney
2. psalm
3. tutor
4. unite
5. dentist
6. valet
7. raw
8. tuxedo
9. eject
10. zoology

Letter Hunt #14, page 72

1. petrified
2. protect
3. journey
4. rogue
5. inspect
6. depot
7. expert
8. shove
9. drill
10. tongue

Answer Key *(cont.)*

Vocabulary Hunt, page 73

chapters 1–2 word: indecent

chapters 3–4 word: hollowness

chapter 5 word: velvet

chapters 6–7 word: cautiously

chapter 8 word: repeated

chapters 9–10 word: sauntered

Novel Hunt, page 74

1. $225.00
2. well, water, fountain
3. lawyer
4. 80th, 5th, Madison, 42nd
5. New York, museum, bus, Connecticut
6. macaroni, cheese
7. bathroom
8. Angel
9. three
10. Florence, Italy

Style Hunt, page 74

an idiom in Chapter One:
"Oh, Baloney!"

Vocabulary Hunt, page 75

chapters 1–4 word: gnats

chapters 5–8 word: wandering

chapters 9–12 word: peculiar

chapters 13–16 word: legal

chapters 17–20 word: fraction

chapters 21–25 word: anxious

Novel Hunt, page 76

1. horse, gnat, toad, fish
2. 87
3. jail
4. hot, humid, sticky
5. any person listed in the obituaries
6. pond, jail, house, woods, forest
7. Mae, Miles, Jesse, Winnie
8. poor, fat
9. pancakes, bacon
10. yellow

Style Hunt, page 76

analogy in the prologue: a Ferris wheel is compared to the life cycle.

Vocabulary Hunt, page 77

chapter 1 word: current

chapter 2 word: horizon

chapter 3 word: possession

chapter 4 word: seized

chapter 5 word: waning

chapter 5 word: pursuers

Novel Hunt, page 78

1. boar, pig
2. Pacific Ocean island
3. bird
4. shark, fish
5. canoe
6. dog
7. spear, knife
8. water
9. bananas
10. north, south

Style Hunt, page 78

native words:

1. ghost spirit
2. paths of the sea
3. bananas
4. shark
5. canoe
6. wild pig
7. pole
8. fish
9. house
10. God of the fisherman

Vocabulary Hunt, page 79

chapters 1–3 word: reins

chapters 4–6 word: ointments

chapters 7–9 word: hypnotized

chapters 10–12 word: mock

chapters 13–14 word: infinite

chapters 15–16 word: immediately

Novel Hunt, page 80

1. plates, cups, etc.
2. cupboard, house, yard
3. little or bear
4. Patrick, Adiel, Little, Omri,
5. horse, rope, saddle, gun
6. thread, twigs, plants
7. food
8. horse from want ads
9. a picture of something a

Native American uses

10. steak, beans, coffee, eggs

Style Hunt, page 80

stereotype in Chapter Ten: Them Injuns isn't jest ornery and savage. Them's dirty.

Vocabulary Hunt, page 81

Part One word: roughhouse

Part One word: morsel

Part Two word: ignored

Part Two word: encyclopedia

Part Three word: lemon-yellow

Part Three word: constellations

Novel Hunt, page 82

1. San Francisco
2. wilderness
3. meat, caribou, animals, mice
4. independent, gentle, aggressive, protective
5. a town in Alaska
6. fur, gun, knife, dogs, etc.
7. north
8. grass, snow, lichens, animals
9. caribou
10. a picture of a tree, etc.

Style Hunt, page 82

descriptive words:

1. hardy flowers
2. thaws briefly
3. rigorous land
4. bountiful flowers
5. large clouds
6–10 Answers may vary

Vocabulary Hunt, page 83

chapters 1–2 word: meddle

chapters 3–4 word: grownups

chapters 5–6 word: underdogs

chapters 7–8 word: population

chapters 9–10 word: ambush

chapters 11–13 word: epidemic

Novel Hunt, page 84

1. Sam, Jerry, William, Tim
2. rifle, musket, gun
3. Massachusetts, Connecticut
4. red
5. British, England, King

Answer Key *(cont.)*

6. Redding, Lexington, Concord
7. Adams, Arnold, Burke, Hancock
8. cow
9. 16–18
10. horse, buggy, wagon

Style Hunt, page 84
metaphor in Chapter 12: They're animals now; they're all beasts.

Vocabulary Hunt, page 85
chapters 1–3 word: massive
chapters 4–6 word: chocolate
chapters 7–9 word: flammable
chapters 10–13 word: golden
chapters 14–16 word: concentrate
chapters 17–19 word: exhaustion

Novel Hunt, page 86
1. wing, propeller, fuselage
2. L
3. United States, Canada
4. eggs
5. hamburger, milkshake
6. moose, porcupine, fish, bear, wolf, mosquito
7. dawn, dusk, morning, evening
8. Gary
9. food, gun, radio
10. drill bit

Style Hunt, page 86
repeated words: divorce, mistakes, the secret

Vocabulary Hunt, page 87
chapters 1–4 word: coaxed
chapters 5–9 word: schoolroom
chapters 10–13 word: discarding
chapters 14–17 word: disappeared
chapters 18–22 word: ancient
chapters 23–25 word: supper

Novel Hunt, Page 88
1. deer, squirrel, bear
2. spear
3. Maine
4. gun, watch
5. Ben

6. meat, corn, fish
7. dog
8. bees
9. bear
10. Sarah

Style Hunt, page 88
dialect in Chapter Three: mebbe

Vocabulary Hunt, page 89
chapters 1–2 word: resentment
chapters 3–4 word: fragrance
chapters 5–6 word: pavement
chapters 7–8 word: somber
chapters 9–10 word: nightmares
chapters 11–12 word: dissolved

Novel Hunt, page 90
1. space, stars, astronomy
2. rainy, cold, windy
3. Mrs. and who
4. dog
5. red
6. It
7. poorly
8. planet, space, earth, house
9. planet
10. basketball

Style Hunt, Page 90
Accept any of the proverbs from the story.

Vocabulary Hunt, page 91
chapters 1–3 word: inevitable
chapters 4–5 word: occasionally
chapters 6–8 word: precisely
chapters 9–12 word: despise
chapters 13–16 word: immense
chapters 17–22 word: scarlet

Novel Hunt, page 92
1. gin, alcohol
2. dark, black, blue
3. Baby
4. champion
5. cars, automobiles
6. apple
7. England, Great Britain
8. mean
9. leg

10. Danny, William, Enoch, Victor

Style Hunt, page 92
onomatopoeia in Chapter 12: *clink*, and Chapter 16: *thump*

Vocabulary Hunt, page 93
chapters 1–3 word: gaze
chapters 4–6 word: centipedes
chapters 7–10 word: slingshot
chapters 11–13 word: green
chapters 14–17 word: versatile
chapters 18–22 word: trembled

Novel Hunt, page 94
1. animals, tractor, barn
2. Wilbur, Charlotte, Templeton
3. horses, cows, children, rides
4. barn
5. cow, spider, pig, rat
6. White
7. rat
8. web
9. spring
10. bacon, ham, pork chops

Style Hunt, page 94
The story is a fantasy because the animals talk.

Vocabulary Hunt, page 95
chapters 1–5 word: pelt
chapters 6–10 word: beckoned
chapters 11–15 word: gnawed
chapters 16–20 word: ledge
chapters 21–25 word: whiskers
chapters 26–29 word: stranded

Novel Hunt, page 96
1. trout, cod, halibut, etc.
2. cliffs, rocks, ravine, etc.
3. a place in Russia
4. Pacific
5. ship
6. a picture of an island on a map
7. any blue object
8. dog
9. windy, warm, etc.

Answer Key *(cont.)*

10. North Star, Polaris

Style Hunt, page 96

metaphor in Chapter Two: It is a flat stone.

personification in Chapter Seven: rocks that guard

onomatopoeia in Chapter 19: reep, reep

simile in Chapter 21: like a snake

Vocabulary Hunt, page 97

chapters 1–2 word: energetic

chapter 3 word: bonnet

chapter 4 word: silk

chapter 5 word: pitchfork

chapters 6–7 word: dandelions

chapters 8–9 word: stubbornly

Novel Hunt, page 98

1. blue, gray, green
2. cat
3. red, green
4. horse, sheep
5. house, plains, pond
6. Caleb, Anna, Sarah
7. cooking, cutting hair
8. Maine
9. pencils
10. yellow

Style Hunt, page 98

personification in Chapter One: prairie reached out and touched the sky

Vocabulary Hunt, page 99

chapters 1–2 word: discard

chapters 3–4 word: grudgingly

chapters 5–6 word: trio

chapters 7–8 word: trickle

chapters 9–10 word: beige

chapters 11–13 word: constricting

Novel Hunt, page 100

1. sadness, love
2. football
3. cow
4. a bridge
5. large

6. teacher
7. Jesse, Janice, Leslie
8. art, drawing
9. house, school, Washington, D.C.
10. dog

Style Hunt, page 100

simile in Chapter Four: like one of the strings

personification in Chapter Four: Dogwood and redwood played hide and seek.

metaphor in Chapter Five: "He'd have to fight the female gorilla now."

onomatopoeia in Chapter Eight: plink, plink

idiom in Chapter Eight: fit to fry

Vocabulary Hunt, page 101

chapter 1 word: passengers

chapter 2 word: degrees

chapter 3 word: whizzed

chapter 4 word: feathery

chapter 5 word: postpone

chapter 6 word: curb

Novel Hunt, page 102

1. orange
2. bus
3. home, house, bedroom, outside
4. meat, bone, dog food
5. police
6. any breed of dog
7. 35 cents
8. Henry, Huggins, etc.
9. bully, mean
10. cow, sheep

Style Hunt, page 102

derogatory language in Chapter Six: "Aw, you're just a dumb girl."

Vocabulary Hunt, page 103

chapters 1–3 word: hoax

chapters 4–6 word: spectacles

chapters 7–9 word: throne

chapters 10–12 word: breeze

chapters 13–15 word: forfeit

chapters 16–17 word: quarry

Novel Hunt, page 104

1. Lucy, Edmund, Peter
2. kind, elderly, old
3. clothes, etc.
4. house, forest, castle
5. none or zero
6. snow
7. brave, independent, leader
8. lion, beaver
9. which
10. picture of Lucy from the comics

Style Hunt, page 104

sarcasm in Chapter 11: "Are you my councilor or my slave?"

Vocabulary Hunt, page 105

chapters 1–4 word: mustangs

chapters 5–8 word: whispered

chapters 9–12 word: naked

chapters 13–17 word: crawled

chapters 18–22 word: porridge

chapters 23–26 word: notion

Novel Hunt, page 106

1. grass, flowers, soil
2. dog
3. corn, berries, grass, hay, wheat, etc.
4. Laura, Mary, Carrie, Caroline, etc.
5. well
6. Kansas, Nebraska, the Dakotas, Oklahoma
7. berries, corn bread, milk, steak
8. horse
9. rabbit, wolf, mustang, fox, bird
10. brave, kind, humorous

Style Hunt, page 106

hyperbole in Chapter 15: must weigh forty pounds and I'm weak as water.

Vocabulary Hunt, page 107

chapters 1–3 word: mischief

chapters 4–6 word: cutthroat

chapters 7–8 word: orphan

chapters 9–12 word: ransom

Answer Key *(cont.)*

chapters 13–16 word: starve

chapters 17–19 word: ignorance

Novel Hunt, page 108
1. brave, mature, independent
2. garlic, fruit, bread, herring
3. Jemmy, Billy, Betsy
4. bear
5. sewer, log
6. forest, river
7. gold, jewels
8. prince, queen, king
9. synonym for whip
10. spoiled brat, baby, immature

Style Hunt, page 108
simile in Chapter One: yowl like a stuck pig

Vocabulary Hunt, page 109
chapters 1–3 word: ceiling

chapters 4–6 word: accompany

chapters 7–9 word: delicate

chapters 10–12 word: scrubbing

chapters 13–15 word: masons

chapters 16–17 word: innocent

Novel Hunt, page 110
1. cat, horse, cow, pig
2. red
3. Q
4. birth, baby
5. cat
6. Alyce, Kate, Jane, Robert, Thomas, John
7. eggs, bread, milk, herring, almond, pork, ale, pudding
8. yellow
9. village, river, manor
10. poor

Style Hunt, page 110
alliteration in Chapter Nine: moaning mewling mound

Vocabulary Hunt, page 111
chapter 1 word: metamorphosed

chapter 2 word: cunningly

chapter 3 word: summit

chapter 4 word: dawn

chapter 5 word: heartbreaking

chapters 6–7 word: contemplate

Novel Hunt, page 112
1. knife
2. cold, wet, harsh
3. caribou, moose, fish, meat
4. sled
5. fish, meat
6. Hans, John, Pete
7. river, ocean, island, Russia, Yukon, Canada
8. wild, fast
9. dog
10. north or northwest (in U.S.)

Style Hunt, page 112
style elements in Chapter Seven:

idiom: lost his head

simile: arrows like a porcupine

metaphor: live hurricane

hyperbole: hair leap straight on his neck

Word Trees, page 117
1. ad, had (an, and)
2. me, met
3. he, her, here
4. do, old, loud
5. *or*, for (or, rot) *or* (of, for) *or* to, rot